The Three Women Who Changed My Life

John W. Cronin

Independently published

Editing, print layout, e-book conversion,
and cover design by DLD Books
Editing and Self-Publishing Services

DLD Books
www.dldbooks.com

Copyright 2025 by John W. Cronin
All rights reserved.

Cover photo of John, his wife, his mother, and his sister
was taken in 1996.

ISBN: 9798308485841

The Three Women Who Changed My Life

Acknowledgements

I would like to thank my mother, who gave me the skills to navigate the world. Her unconditional love and attention enabled me to overcome the rough patches in my life. She refused to send me to an institution for the victims of polio, although it made her life more difficult.

I must apologize to my sister, Anne, for monopolizing far more than my fair share of Mother's love and affection. My polio and operations controlled much of Mother's time, denying Anne the attention she deserved.

This book would not be possible if it were not for my wife, Gillian. She helps me with every facet of life, even writing. She is there to hold my hand every time a medical emergency arises. Her companionship and care have kept me out of institutions.

Thanks are also due to Winslow Parker, who read and commented on every chapter of the book. I learned so much from him. I also want to thank the writing collective Behind Our Eyes for providing a venue where I could showcase my work and gain some writing help.

I must also thank my editors, Leonore and David Dvorkin

of DLD Books. They made my dream of publishing my memoir come true. I could never have accomplished it without their help. The story benefited greatly from their skill.

1
Early Life

I knew my parents wanted and loved me because they adopted me. If they had not wanted a child, they would not have adopted. That's how I ended up on a farm in southern Ontario, six months after my birth, on October 10, 1955.

Living on a farm was wonderful for a boy of my temperament, as it provided plenty of space for an exuberant child to run around. The barn and shed were places for exploration and adventure. There were all types of farm equipment for me to climb on, over, and under. Dog, cats, piglets, and calves were my playmates.

If Daddy planned to use the tractor, I pestered him to allow me to sit on the seat and ride with him. If the weather was inclement or the task too dangerous, Mom played the heavy by prohibiting me from riding. For me, Daddy could do no wrong.

Visitors called me Daddy's shadow. Wherever he went, John was sure to follow. Daddy tucked me in at night with my toy tractor and promises of adventures the next day. At night, I dreamed that Daddy and I rode on a tractor. I knew that when I grew big like him, I would be a farmer and drive a big, red Massey-Harris tractor.

One day, while I was playing at helping with the barn

chores, Daddy gave me an important job. I was to carry the syringe full of medication from the milk house to Daddy. Curious to see what happened if I pushed the plunger, I did, and all that expensive medication disappeared into the straw. It was a long time before Daddy trusted me again with an important job.

My favorite game was having Daddy squirt warm milk from the cow's teat into my mouth. We worked as a team, with him aiming and me catching. No matter how hard we tried, I always ended up with a creamy white mustache.

In 1958, a small bundle made a big change in our lives. A baby girl joined our happy family. I had a sister. Mom couldn't keep me away from her.

"Mom, look at Anne's tiny fingers and toes. She's so pretty! Can I kiss her? Can I hold her? When she gets big, we can play."

"Yes, you can play when Anne gets older, but you can't hold her. You might drop her. But you can give her a big kiss on her forehead."

The next year, while we were threshing, an incident happened that showed how quickly a non-threatening situation can spiral out of control and become dangerous. The threshing machine is a large, noisy, belt-driven monster with numerous open, high-speed pulleys. When the machine is separating the grain from the straw, the suffocating dust makes everything appear murky. While it's in operation, the pounding of the machine as it shakes the grain loose makes the barn floor vibrate, making speech impossible. To prevent things going awry, the owner of the machine is continually walking around and on the machine, ensuring that everything is running smoothly. As he was the owner of the machine, this job fell to my uncle Morris.

Unthinking, I followed Uncle Morris as he climbed atop the quaking threshing machine to make some adjustments. While he was on top of the shuddering, noisy beast, a hunch told him to turn around—whereupon, like an apparition, I materialized from the curtain of yellowish-brown dust. The shock of seeing me almost caused Uncle Morris to topple from his perch on the threshing machine. Dumbfounded at the sight of me, he could not imagine how I had found my way onto the machine. More important, how was he going to get me safely back to earth?

Not wanting to frighten me, he bent down, grabbed my shoulders, and turned me around, while yelling into my ear and pointing to the rear of the bucking beast. Slowly we crept to the rear of the machine and climbed down the ladder, coming to rest on the plank barn floor.

Although I was now safe, Uncle Morris continued shaking like a leaf. I had no idea why, but I knew there was something wrong by the way he clenched his teeth, trying to hold in his anger, as he spat out, "Go to the house immediately! I'll deal with you later!"

These minor scrapes did nothing to lessen my joy in farm life. I was living the Canadian dream. Little did I know that the untroubled days of the summer of 1959 marked an end to our peaceful, stable, joyous life.

2
Polio

"Mom, can I go out to the barn with Daddy after supper?"

"No! You were out all afternoon. Ever since you came in for supper, you've complained about aches and pains. You usually ask for more, but this evening you didn't finish your supper. Come over here. Let me feel your forehead. Hmm, you feel warm. I think you might have the flu. I'm going to take your temperature. You have a fever of 101! Young man, I think you'll be keeping me company this evening."

"Ah, Mom, I feel all right. I only want to stay out for a little while."

"It's bath time. Get in the bathroom and undress. Don't think about giving me any back talk. Into the tub with you. You can play while I clean the bathroom."

"Play time is over. Stand up so I can scrub you clean."

"I can't stand up! My legs don't work. What's wrong with me, Mom?"

"Calm down. Stop the crying. We'll get you dressed, and

then it's off to the doctor's office."

Turning to Mary, the teacher who boarded with us, Mom said, "Mary, since you don't teach tomorrow, could you look after Anne until we return? Wally, you can carry John out to the car. We have to take him to Doctor Lahey's surgery." Whispering to Daddy, she said, "I think it's polio. I pray I'm wrong."

After some poking and prodding, Doctor Lahey said, "I carried out a preliminary exam. It appears that he has some paralysis, but still, it may only be the flu, I hope. Take him to the Victoria Hospital in London." (That was London, Canada.) "They'll be able to confirm the diagnosis."

"Hello, Mr. and Mrs. Cronin. To confirm our diagnosis of John's medical problem, we have to perform a spinal tap. The nurse will slide the needle between the vertebrae, drawing off some spinal fluid for testing. It won't take long."

When I saw the syringe with the long needle, I started crying, calling out, "Mom, don't let them stick that thing into me! It'll hurt!"

It did hurt, but that was only the beginning of what would turn out to be months of pain and horror. Whisked away from Mom and Daddy by gowned attendants, I couldn't stop sobbing. Deposited in an isolation room, I no longer had contact with real people. The delirium and the drugs consigned me to a dreamland of pain and loss.

Ephemeral, white–draped doctors and nurses drifted in and out of my fevered dream world like ghosts. Pain was a constant companion as the polio virus burned out individual nerves.

At times, apparitions floated into my cell, injecting me with opiates, hoping to keep the pain at bay. At other times, the specters arrived with a cabinet containing hot packs, which they put on my joints, trying to assuage the pain. After every attempt at mitigation, the returning pain was worse.

The lack of human contact intensified my already frightening situation. Being ripped from the bosom of my loving family at the age of four and thrust into an isolation room left me bewildered. Apparitions drifting in and out of the isolation chamber attended to me, but there was no human contact. Gowns and rubber gloves prevented skin-to-skin contact. Fear of contracting the virus kept the staff from touching, holding, or cuddling me

For me, no physical contact with Mom or Daddy was heartbreaking. Even gloved, gowned, and masked, they could not enter my isolation cell. In order to visit, they stood on a bench outside the room's one window. Rain, shine, sleet, or snow, they stood on the bench, trying to comfort me. Because of the window placement, I could not see Mom or Dad, and hearing them was difficult. Although Mom visited every day, my inability to see or touch her left me feeling lonely and abandoned.

Later, I learned that my isolation cell had previously done duty as a TB isolation ward in the 1920s and '30s.

One day a doctor and his entourage appeared, telling me, "John, you're no longer contagious. This means you can move from the isolation room to a general ward with other patients. Your parents will be able to visit with you."

"Oh, yes! I miss them so much! Can I take my stuffed animals with me? They've been my best friends since I've been in here."

"No, they may still hold germs. It's better if we destroy them."

Lying in bed with my eyes glued to the entrance to my new, large, cheery ward, I was excited, waiting for my visitors.

Suddenly they appeared. I was ecstatic.

"Mom! Daddy!" I cried out. "I'm over here! Can you see me? I love you!" I was on cloud nine.

"My Johnny! I'm so glad to hold you. Here's a big hug from Anne and me. Daddy's got another big hug for you."

"I'm so happy you're here. I was so lonely. I cried every day."

"You don't need to worry anymore, Johnny. One of us will visit you every day until they release you."

On one of his visits, the doctor told his entourage, "The polio may cause muscles to contract. This may cause the limbs to deform. To prevent this, we'll put John's legs into an open cast."

Without consulting my parents, they placed open casts with no cotton padding on my legs.

After a few days I complained, "Nurse, my feet and legs are sore. The pain is getting worse. Please do something."

"There's nothing to worry about. The casts will keep your legs straight. It's for your own good."

"Hi, Mom! I'm so glad you're here. No one will listen to me. Look at my legs and feet. They hurt. I told the nurse, and she did nothing."

"Let Mom see. I'll be gentle. My gosh! Your leg and heel are a mass of open sores. We won't put up with this."

Off to the nursing station my champion marched.

With a nurse in tow, Mom demanded, "Look at those open, festering sores. How could this happen? Does no one care about my son?"

"I told them, Mom, but no one listened."

"Nurse Smith, get something to relieve the pain and start to clean up these raw sores. I don't want to hear that you can't remove the casts without the doctor's permission. Before you think about putting John's legs into cast again, make sure all the sores have healed and the casts are thoroughly padded. I don't want to come and find neglect like this again. I wish medical personnel would listen and not just think that children are whining."

The next step on the road to recovery was my move from the Victoria Hospital to the London Children's Hospital. Here I underwent assessment and rehabilitation training. Daily, physiotherapists exercised my legs, hoping to maintain muscle mass and possibly stimulate some motion. They wanted to determine to what degree I retained motor control over my muscles. They used massage in an attempt to mitigate the joint pains.

The next step in the rehabilitation program was choosing crutches and having leg braces custom made. To accomplish this, they wheeled me to what I later thought of as Santa's magic workshop for broken children. The workshop was alive with the babble of voices, the squeal of stainless steel as it was cut and ground, and the smell of new leather and oil. From a few lines on some butcher paper, they fashioned new legs for me. With stainless steel, leather, and padding, these artisans gave me the precious gift of walking. Truly, this was a magic workshop for damaged children.

It didn't take long before I was hopping around on my new legs. They taught me to walk one foot at a time, but the bunny hop was much faster. The art of falling without injury and how to recover after a fall were two more lessons I needed to learn.

"Mrs. Cronin, when John returns home with you, try to

ensure that you exercise and massage his legs with some heat at least once a day. That will help with the pain. Have him walk every day to strengthen his muscles. Make sure he eats a high-fiber diet. Being a paraplegic, John will be more prone to constipation. Because paraplegics live a more sedentary life than the average person does, the walking motion that helps food move through the intestine is absent. He'll have to be careful with his diet for the remainder of his life. That's why it's important to get him accustomed to eating a high-fiber diet when he's young."

I thought the physiotherapists were tough taskmasters until I returned home and Mom took over my physio. Rain or shine, she made sure I walked every morning and afternoon. Twice a day, Mom exercised my legs and feet. Every evening, she massaged my legs, trying to lessen the joint pain. She did everything in her power to help me regain control of my body.

Repeatedly, as I grew older, I asked myself, "Why me?" Although I had taken the three separate vaccinations, I still contracted polio. Later, I learned that the efficacy of some of the batches was questionable. Did the vaccine give me polio, or did it only fail to protect me? I don't know, but either way, it did protect many other children from the dread disease.

Since the past could not be changed, Mother was determined I would live a normal life despite the polio. With her help, Anne and I went fishing. No fancy rod, just a bamboo pole with a line, hook, and sinker. On other occasions, the swimming pool was our destination. Mom sat watching Anne and me as we frolicked in the children's pool. This is where I learned to swim before graduating to the big pool.

With braces, crutches, and a wheelchair, I attended grade school, high school, and university with no special adaptations made. My paralysis and poor vision didn't hinder me in my travels in foreign lands. I was determined to never allow myself to become a burden, while pushing myself to do whatever a "normal" person would.

Note

For further information on polio, go here:
https://en.wikipedia.org/wiki/Polio

3
The Wake

"John, Anne, I have something important to tell you. Daddy is too sick to run the farm any longer. We have to sell the farm and move into Teeswater."

"But Mom," I said, "I don't want to leave the farm! I don't know what Teeswater will be like."

"I understand that you don't want to leave everything you're familiar with, but we have no choice. The sale is next week, and we'll move the week after. Your Uncle Morris and some of the neighbors will help."

"Will the kids in town want to be my friends? Will they be mean? What about my cousins Joe and Marianne? Will I still get to play with them?"

Hugging us to her breast like little chicks, Mom soothed us. "Don't worry. Everything will work out. You'll find new friends. Like now, you'll still see your cousins Joe, Marianne, and Theresa. Whenever Aunt Regina comes into town to shop, she'll drop them off for a visit."

With tears welling up, Anne hiccupped, "I'm not going. I'm scared. We're safe here."

"Don't worry, Anne. There'll be girls for you to play with. It won't take long for you and John to make new friends."

"I won't get to play on the tractors and in the barn," I said. "I'll have to stay in the house all the time."

"No, John. Getting around town will be much easier. You'll have sidewalks and paved roads to wheel around on."

Sure enough, two weeks later, our yard filled with neighbors hoping for a bargain or just browsing. They sold the big red Massey-Harris tractor I loved. All my animal friends except for the cats went on the auction block. Everything we had taken for granted was about to be sold.

The next week, all our remaining possessions were loaded on wagons and hauled to our new rental house in Teeswater. I felt sad leaving all my familiar surroundings, but there was always hope that things would improve

After a couple of weeks, before we had fully settled, Mom hugged Anne and me to her, and with tears welling up, she broke the terrible news. "Daddy died. He'll no longer be with us. He's gone home to Jesus."

Mom's sorrow washed over us, causing Anne and me to weep. With tears running down her cheeks, Anne said, "I'll never see Daddy again? Who will lift me up to the sky? Are you sure he's gone?"

"Yes, I'm sure. Daddy is gone. Now you and John go out to play and leave Mom alone."

When Anne and I left the house, I heard Mom sobbing as grief overwhelmed her. Not fully understanding what had occurred and what Mom was going through, I decided to inform the neighbors. Going from house to house, I knocked on doors, giving each householder the news. I felt important.

The next day, black curtains hung at the windows, giving the rooms a gloomy, somber atmosphere. With the bier placed in front of the bow windows and red votive candles burning at each end of the casket, Daddy was ready to receive the mourners.

Before any of the bereaved arrived, Mom brought us in to say goodbye to Daddy. Standing on the plush padded kneeler, I held Daddy's cold dry hand as I whispered a prayer.

Lifting Anne up to see Daddy, Mom asked, "Can you see Daddy? Take his hand. Would you like to give him a goodbye kiss?"

"No. He's too cold."

That evening, the mourners commenced arriving. Everyone proceeded to the front room to pay their respects to Daddy and pray for his soul. When they had paid their respects, the visitors retired to the kitchen to share food, drink, and conversation.

Anne and I naturally gravitated to the kitchen, where everything took place. Being the recipients of everyone's sympathy, we were the center of attention until Mom sent us to bed.

The day of the funeral, Mom had too many problems to worry about Anne and me. To help Mom get through the day, the local health nurse brought us to her home. This woman was a rock for Mom to lean on and indispensable when it came to getting help for me. In the past, she had arranged for me to get a wheelchair and glasses.

At the time, I didn't understand what Daddy's loss meant to me personally and the family in general. His death destroyed all our hopes, dreams, and plans for the future. Mom's dream of a life surrounded by her loving, caring husband and children fell to pieces. Any hope that Anne could live a normal life, with parents that had time to shower her with the love she deserved, dissolved with Daddy's passing. His demise dashed any plans I had of becoming a farmer and driving a big red tractor like him. The future felt frightening.

4
Teeswater

Shooting down the green door we used as a ramp in the rented house, I felt like a bull coming out of the chute at the Calgary Stampede. Mom was right. These concrete sidewalks were perfect for me to whizz around town. With very little traffic on the side streets, I could also use the roads to reach places not served by sidewalks. The gravel and rough, grassy surroundings of the farm would no longer hamper my freedom of movement.

At first, uncertain about our new surroundings, Anne and I stuck close to the house. However, it didn't take long before we found a cadre of friends. When our gang of little rascals trooped through town, adults waved and called out friendly greetings.

"Let's go exploring!" someone shouted, and explore we did. Where? Anywhere, everywhere. We were off, wandering the roads, lanes, and parks of Teeswater. It was not long before town became an open book for our gang of little scamps.

When I was bored with exploring, I challenged Anne. "Hey, Anne. Wanna race? See how fast you can get your new green trike going."

"No! I don't want to race you. You're bigger than me. That's not fair. Find someone else."

I did. Whenever I met someone with a tricycle or bicycle, I

asked, "Do you want to race? We can line up on the road. When I say go, we all go. One, two, three, *go!*" And we were off. Pumping the wheels with all my might, I outran the tricycles, but I couldn't outrace the bicycles.

After one loss to a bicyclist, I asked, "What makes the clicking sound I hear coming from your wheels?"

"Trading cards. I stick them in the spokes. The more cards, the faster the sounds come. It doesn't quite sound like the growl of a race car, but it's good enough for me!"

"I sure would like that sound for my wheelchair, but I don't have any cards."

"Here," he said, taking a card from his bike and fixing it in place on my wheelchair. "That should do it. All right."

"What player is on the trading card?"

"Who else but Johnny Bower? The greatest goalie the Maple Leafs ever had. Come on. Start your engine. Let's go!"

"All right! That's great. He's my hero. Let's go. I'm ready to race."

One afternoon, while I was wheeling along the cracked sidewalk near our house, our neighbor's son cried out, "Hey, Four Eyes! Can you see through those Coke bottle bottoms? You think you're special when your friends are pushing you around in the stupid chair. Now your friends aren't around to help you!"

"I'm not afraid of you," I retorted. "Come on, and I'll fight you. If I grab you, I'll squeeze you until you poop. I've got bigger muscles than you."

"You don't scare me. I'll show you." My tormenter picked up a stone. "I'll fix you!"

Unable to dodge the missile, I cried out in pain when the rock hit my chin. "You bully! Why did you do that? Look at what you did. I'm bleeding."

Rushing into the house, I cried out, "Mom! I'm bleeding! The Johnson kid threw a stone at me. See? I'm bleeding. He got me just below my lips."

"Let me see. It doesn't look too bad. Stay still while I press this cold damp cloth on the cut."

"Why did he throw the stone at me, Mom?"

"Some people are bullies, Johnny. A person bullied at home may take out his anger on those he perceives to be weaker. He threw the stone because he was afraid of your strength."

"But I don't like fighting, Mom."

"That's good, but sometimes, when you meet a bully that insists on a fight, you have to stand up for yourself. However, always try to avoid fighting if you can. I'll talk to his father. He may get a spanking, but that will only make him angrier."

The start of the new school year found us living in a brand-spanking new yellow-brick bungalow. Mom drew the blueprints and oversaw the construction, making sure the house was completely wheelchair accessible. The lot Mom chose was less than a block from school and church, making it easy for me to wheel there.

Although school was close, I began to dread wheeling there.

"Hey, Four Eyes! Are you blind, or just ugly? Why are you in that stupid chair? Cripple, cripple, can't catch me!"

"Stop that!" I demanded. "I'll tell the teacher."

"Look at the baby. Gonna cry, baby? Run and tattle to the teacher. Teacher's pet. Crybaby."

"I'll fight you! Come closer!"

"No, you won't. You can't catch me. If the teacher sees you, he'll give you the strap." They laughed, dancing around me.

Every morning as I prepared for school, I became anxious thinking about the gauntlet of taunts I had to face.

"Mom, why are they so mean? I didn't do anything to them. They hate me."

"No, John. They don't hate you. They pick on you because you're different."

"That's not my fault. It's the polio."

"You're right, John. They tease you because they want to see you become upset and angry. When they make you miserable, they're happy. Some children are cruel, while others tease you trying to divert attention from themselves. The best way to beat the taunts of bullies is to laugh with them. When you laugh with them instead of becoming angry, they don't know how to react. If you continue to laugh with them, they'll become bored and move on to another victim."

That day, armed with Mom's advice, I faced down the enemy.

"Cripple, cripple, get out of the chair," they taunted, cavorting just outside my reach.

"No! It's fun wheeling around. Everyone walks, while I get to ride. Do you want to try? Stand on the two pipes sticking out the back of the wheelchair."

One of the less belligerent bullies broke ranks and stepped onto the pipes extending from the wheelchair. Leaning forward, I pushed hard on the wheels, causing us to fly along the sidewalk. Soon all my tormentors were vying for a ride on the back of the wheelchair. Mom's advice had worked.

Being close to school and church was not nearly as important to me as was the big hill in front of the house.

"Wow, Anne! Check out the hill. I could get going real fast down this steep hill. Come on, let's race."

"No. It looks too steep. We could get hit by a car."

"Don't worry, Anne. I'll be careful and go slow the first time. I want to get the feel of the hill before I shoot down."

Gingerly, Anne and I coasted down the steep hill, with her on her bright green trike and me in the wheelchair.

Reaching the bottom, I said to myself, "This is going to be lots of fun. I'll be able to shoot down the hill like a bullet. However, I've got to be extra careful that I don't get hit by a car at the corner."

"Anne, I'm gonna ride down the hill again. This time, I'm gonna zoom down, just like a plane. Coming?"

"No, I'll stay here. I'm tired. I'll watch for cars."

Back up the hill. No brakes on this run, freewheeling all the way. "All right!" I screamed, waving my arms in the air. "See? No hands! I'm gonna take off like a rocket! Anything coming?" I shouted to Anne.

Receiving the all clear from Anne, I shot through the intersection. Wasting no time, I leaned into the hill, pumping the wheels with a will, hurrying to the top for another wild ride.

With the arrival of winter, I was no longer free to roam. I had to stay inside. I could no longer use my glorious hill. I was desolate.

Mom came to our rescue. "John, Anne, do you want to go sledding with me?"

"Oh, yes, Mom! You're the greatest!"

It didn't take long for us to don our boots, coats, mittens, and Christmas tuques—knitted caps to you Americans—and join the other children on the hill.

The Three Women Who Changed My Life

The hard-packed snow was perfect for the narrow steel runners on our sled. On every run, I flew down the hill like a jet, leaving everyone eating my snow. At the bottom, I waited a few minutes while Mom trudged down the hill. She then hauled the sled and me up the hill for another run, whereupon it was another quick trip down the hill. Up and down the hill. She worked like a horse. I didn't appreciate all the work Mom was doing so I could enjoy sledding. All I thought of was the next trip down the hill.

"It's time to go in," she finally told me. "You wore your poor old mom out pulling the sled up the hill. I have to make supper. Get in the house and take those wet clothes off."

"Ah, Mom. Just one more ride. Please! Pretty please!"

"No, John. Stop the whining. I spent the afternoon with you, pulling you up the hill. Your mother needs a break. I have more things to do than pulling you around on the sled."

"I'm sorry. What's for supper?"

With my cousins now in the same school as me, winter and education became fun.

"Come on, John!" cried cousin Tim. "You're done with lunch. Hop on the sled. We have to defend the snow fort. The town kids are trying to take it over."

"No way!" I shouted. "I'll help defend it."

"I made some snowballs for you to throw, John."

Having my cousins with me was so much fun. Every day became a new adventure. For me, life was perfect.

The next spring, I sensed a change. An older, husky, dark-haired man named Frank started coming around, talking with

Mom. On a couple of occasions, he took Mom, Anne, and me for a visit to his farm near Chepstow. On these trips, I met two of his sons, Frank and Larry.

In the barn, we saw dogs, cats, cows, pigs, and horses. Anne couldn't resist playing with the cats and calves. Assured she could ride the workhorses, Anne was on cloud nine. Now that I could no longer run around and play with farm animals, I wasn't impressed with them or the barn.

On the way home, I told myself, "Nice place to visit, but I wouldn't want to live there. Frank and Larry may be good companions, but I would have to leave all my friends and cousins behind." Everything on their farm was grass and gravel. There were no sidewalks or paved roads for me to zoom around on. They still used an outhouse. I didn't want to give up town life and all its conveniences.

You can imagine my surprise when Mom told us, "Anne, John, Frank asked me to marry him. I've accepted."

"What about Daddy?" I asked, very distressed. "Are you just gonna forget him?"

"No, John. I will never forget your father. I loved him with all my heart and soul, but he's no longer with us. Daddy has gone to be with Jesus."

"But Mom, what about our friends? We'll have to leave them," Anne and I whined. "Please, let's stay. We feel safe here. We're tired of moving. We don't know what it will be like there."

"I understand, but I can't go it on my own. Money is short. There's no help from the government."

"But..."

With tears streaking our upturned faces, Mom crushed us to her, trying to keep from weeping.

That night, as I lay in bed thinking about our future, I could hear Mom sobbing into her pillow.

Uncertain about what the future held in store for us left me mixed up. "I don't want to go," I thought, "but Mom needs us to go. Every time things seem to go right, something bad happens. When will we get some good luck? You have no choice, John. For Mom's sake, you have to make the best of the situation."

5
Operations

Polio could have killed me, turned me into a quadriplegic, or relegated me to an iron lung for life. Fortunately, it only made me a paraplegic. The rehabilitation taught me how to live with the paralysis. Every aspect of my life changed when I contracted polio, but I swore to do everything in my power to live a "normal" life.

A person may survive the initial ravages of polio, but polio is a degenerative disease that continues to cause problems for the life of the victim. This occurs because nerve damage prevents signals from the brain from reaching the muscles. Unable to be used, the muscles weaken and atrophy. This allows the tendons to exert an uneven pressure on the bones, which may result in a twisted skeleton. To mitigate any future effects caused by atrophy, I underwent two surgeries.

During one of my biyearly visits to the Children's Hospital in London, while I paraded before numerous doctors and physiotherapists, Dr. Kennedy pointed. "See how he walks hunched over. With his bum thrust back, he walks like a duck. That's because the muscles on either side of the groin are contracting, pulling him forward. We'll make incisions on either side of the groin and lengthen the muscles. For five to six weeks after the surgery you'll be in a full body cast, John, from ankles to nipples."

Petrified, I asked, "How will I pee and poop?"

One of the younger physiotherapists smiled and said reassuringly, "The cast has a square cut out so you can use the bedpan and urinal. Don't worry. We'll take good care of you, John. They'll do the surgery in late September, when it's cooler. The cast should be less irritating then."

After two weeks in grade three, once more I found myself in the hospital. Early in the morning, on my second day in the hospital, Mom accompanied me as the nurses pushed my stretcher to the operating theatre. I felt like a condemned man on the way to the gas chamber. Just before entering the operating room, with tears running down her cheeks, Mom squeezed me, kissing me for possibly the last time. She knew what was in store for me, while I had no idea.

The next thing I knew, I was waking up with Mom at my bedside, holding my hand.

"Mom, I'm burning up," I whispered. "Water."

"Here's some water. Sip it slowly. The heat comes from the plaster. As the plaster hardens, it gives off heat. When it finishes curing, there won't be a problem anymore."

After a couple of weeks lying in the hospital, I was bored. There was nothing physically wrong with me. The only problem was the cast.

On one of Mom's visits, I burst with joy when I heard her say, "We're going home. The Studebaker front seat reclines, so you and your cast will fit. You can stay on the living room couch. That way your friends can visit, especially since you'll be home for your birthday."

"Thanks so much, Mom. It'll be lots more fun at home with you and Anne."

However, my return home was not one long party. Every day, Mom went to school and picked up the day's assignments, returning my completed work. She ensured I completed all the work I had missed while in the hospital. I graduated in the top ten that year.

After six weeks on the living room couch, it was finally time to remove the cast. To have this done, Mom took me to the nearby Wingham Hospital. Zip, zip, and the attendant cut the cast open with a hand-held disc saw. No problem.

Then horrible, horrendous pain. They proceeded to remove sixteen stitches from each side of my groin. The stitches were a mess of dried blood and cotton, embedded in eight weeks of new skin. No painkiller, no freezing, but a hard rubber strap to bite down on. I felt like an eight-year-old soldier told to bite the bullet.

The next stop was a dip in a tub full of very hot water to wash off the blood and cotton while exercising my limbs. Sitting up after eight weeks of being prone caused me to almost faint and vomit. Bending to get into the tub after two months of lying flat had me in excruciating pain. It took two attendants and three tubfuls of hot water to wash me clean.

When it became obvious how stiff I was, Mom admitted, "John, I can't get you in and out of the tub at home without help. There's no one I can turn to for help. I'm sorry, John. You'll have to stay in the hospital for Halloween."

About three years later, on another visit to Dr. Kennedy, while I stood before his entourage of doctors and physiotherapists, he pointed, saying, "See how the spine is beginning to curve? The polio allowed some of the muscles holding the spine in place to weaken. This allows the stronger muscles to exert more force, pulling the spine out of alignment. What I propose doing is a Harrington Instrumental. I'll insert a stainless steel rod on either side of the spine, fusing them to the vertebrae. Are there any questions?"

"When will the surgery take place?" I asked. "Will I be able to go home soon? How long until I'm all better?"

"After the surgery, you'll lie flat on a Stryker bed for two months. You will then receive a formfitting plastic jacket that you'll wear for the next year. After wearing the jacket for two months, you can sit up to eat. After eight months, you can sit up for half a day. In a year, there'll be no more sitting restrictions."

That was a lot of information for an almost eleven-year-old to understand and absorb. The doctor's glib statements about the recovery downplayed what turned out to be eighteen months of misery, confinement, and boredom. Whether I understood what I was getting into or not was of no consequence. September found me preparing for another surgery.

However, this time they applied what appeared to be medieval torture to me, hoping to improve the spine's alignment before surgery. Raising the foot of the bed, they placed pulleys at the head and foot. Cloth harnesses encircled my waist and head, with cords running over the pulleys and attached to six-kilogram (13 lb.) weights. For a few days, every morning and evening, they stretched me until I went for surgery.

Upon waking, this time I was not on fire encased in plaster. However, I did find Mom stationed by my bedside, reassuring me, saying, "I know the pain is terrible, but every day there will be a little less. Patience and prayer will get you through these dark days. Sip some water and don't try to talk. Your throat will be raw from the breathing tube. The extra anesthetic they gave you because the operation took longer than they thought will keep you groggy."

Back in the room, I became acquainted with the Stryker bed. We would have a close relationship for the next eight weeks. The special design of the bed enabled the nurses to turn me, preventing bedsores, while keeping the spine immobilized.

The Stryker bed consisted of a flat, padded board resembling an ironing board, only a little wider. There was a padded piece below my buttocks that they removed when I needed the bedpan. Turning me took a team of nurses. A board, similar to the one I lay on, had a cutout for the head and a harness holding the head steady. The nurses placed the board atop me. They then tightened nuts at each end of the boards, squeezing me between the two boards like a piece of meat pressed between two slices of bread. The nurses then threw a couple of straps around the two boards and yanked hard, making the sandwich even tighter. With a flick of the wrist, they rotated the bed, and I was now face down on the other board, with the harness preventing my head from falling forward.

They repeated this procedure every six hours, every day, for eight weeks. You can imagine how monotonous the process became. For me, the major problem was enduring the tight confinement when they turned me, as I suffer from a mild case of claustrophobia.

With the incision healed, boredom became my number one enemy. Books and television helped to fight off the tedium. In order for me to watch television while lying on my stomach, they placed a mirror on a table below me. With the mirror at the right angle, I could watch television in reverse.

The first break in the boredom came when they fitted me with the plastic jacket. It covered me from my hipbones to my nipples, with lacing up the middle. Once a day, nurses unlaced and spread the plastic jacket, allowing them to wash my chest and stomach. They then turned me over, spreading the pliable plastic jacket until they could remove it. The nurses could now wash my back.

Now that I had the jacket to keep the spine immobilized, it was time I tried to stand. To accomplish this, I had to change from a prone position to standing, with no intermediate sitting or bending. In preparation, two nurses helped me slide to the edge of the bed. In one fluid motion, they rolled me off the bed, bringing me into a standing position.

Helping me to stand was routine for the nurses. The difficulties arose when I was on my feet. They didn't know if I would faint, vomit, or only become dizzy when the blood rushed from my head after two months prone. My luck held: no fainting or vomiting. After I had stood for a few minutes, they returned me to bed.

It wasn't long before they had me standing twice a day and walking around, trying to regain my strength. With my condition improving, Christmas only a couple of weeks away, and Mom able to continue my rehabilitation, they discharged me. Once more, the trusty Studebaker with the reclining seats enabled me to return home.

Life was better at home but more work for Mom. She had to strap my braces on me and stand me up twice a day so I could walk around the house. Every day, she removed the jacket in order to wash my back and chest. At mealtime, Mom helped me eat from a tray. Finally, after a couple of months, I could sit for a short time to eat.

By June, I could sit for half a day. This meant I could attend school part time in September. After Christmas, I could sit for a full day. Being back at school ended the monotony. Never before had I been so glad to be back in school among all my friends.

What I did learn from all the pain and misery of the

operations was that no matter how dark the night, there is always a new dawn. With patience, we defeat darkness.

6
Tractor Driving

Lying on the couch, my new bed, my brain was abuzz with all the problems I had encountered in the move.

"The six steps into the house make it impossible for me to take the wheelchair outside," I told myself. "Even if I could get the wheelchair outside, pushing it on the grass and gravel would be virtually unmanageable. There's no indoor plumbing. Having to walk through the summer kitchen and down a couple of steps into the woodshed to reach the outhouse is extremely difficult for me. I hate having to pee into a bottle and use a commode chair. All the freedom I took for granted is gone. Becoming accustomed to this new life is going to be difficult."

"Mom," I asked, "when will I get to sleep in my bed again? I don't want to sleep on the couch in the parlor anymore. There's no privacy. When will the bathroom be finished?"

"Patience, John. It takes time to collect the money and organize the workers. The carpenter is fixing up the old junk room as your bedroom. When he finishes, you'll be able to move into your new room. He'll also build me some kitchen cupboards and rough in the bathroom. In the spring, when the septic tank is in the ground, the plumber will install the pipes and bathroom fixtures. In another eight months, everything will be back to normal."

Mom's word was good. By the end of the following spring, my bedroom, the kitchen cupboards, the bathroom, and the septic tank were all completed.

What was missing was a ramp. Frank refused to install one.

Zipping around outside in the wheelchair was no longer possible. If I wished to enjoy the great outdoors, I needed to use the crutches and leg braces. Although my ability to roam was restricted, there was a benefit. Using the crutches and leg braces daily built phenomenal arm and chest muscles. I lifted my entire weight with every hop. The leg braces also kept my feet and legs straight. Later in life, when I ceased using the leg braces, my feet and legs became bent and twisted. I stopped using the crutches and leg braces when I became blind, as walking became too difficult.

My upper body strength gave me the ability to perform feats of strength that my peers couldn't match. No one could best me at arm wrestling or rope climbing, not even the teacher. My strength enabled me to play hockey, although I skated around on a sled. I used my hands to propel myself over the ice and pass the puck and even had my hands whacked when those on skates checked me. If I hadn't had the strength I did, the barn would not have been nearly as much fun as it had turned out to be. Hand over hand, I climbed the 30-foot ladder to the top of the haymow, where we built our forts. At other times, I swung on a rope, letting go and landing in a pile of straw.

However, most of my play took place in the house. Since Frank Jr. had chores and schoolwork, he was not a constant playmate. Anne should have been the obvious choice for a companion, but young boys didn't generally play with girls. I didn't want Larry or Frank to tease me for playing with her. Sometimes, to avoid the taunts of my older brothers, I mocked Anne. At other times, I was downright cruel to her. I had to save face, and that came at her expense. To this very day, I deeply regret the unkind treatment I heaped on Anne. There is no excuse. The only explanation is that harmony did not exist at the top, and that allowed family relationships to become warped.

There was always tension running through Mom and Frank's relationship over who controlled what. Frank, being the man, thought he should be in charge. Mom would not turn control of her assets or her children over to him. This didn't sit well with him. Two bosses did not make for a harmonious situation.

From the very beginning, Frank could not accept that I was a paraplegic. He saw me as an indulged child who used his medical problems to avoid responsibilities. To a certain extent, I did use my disability that way, but his preoccupation with "straightening me up" was counterproductive. Instead of Mom disciplining me, she protected me from Frank's tongue lashings. If he had let me alone, Mom would have stepped in, taking responsibility for correcting me when that was needed.

With the move came attending a new school and all the fears inherent in meeting new children. Having a brother, sister, and numerous cousins attending the same school eased my apprehension.

Because of the steps in the old school, I couldn't join the other grade four students. Although one of the teachers would not relinquish her classroom, she did consent to teach me. I was the only grade four student among all her grade five and six pupils.

This accommodated my scholarly pursuits, but playing outside was severely curtailed. The playground consisted of a gravel parking lot with a lower, grassy play field that was marshy at times. With no concrete for me to wheel around on, my recess was restricted to watching my peers play.

This lasted for a year. I missed the next school year due to surgery. The following year, I returned to a brand spanking new school. It had sidewalks, a paved parking lot, and a driveway with only one step. Recess became fun. I joined my friends playing touch football, marbles, and tag. Surmounting the one step was easy with help from my friends.

Although life seemed to be looking up, I still felt restricted at home. I needed a ride when I wanted to visit friends. Since there was no bus, someone had to drive me the mile and a quarter to school. However, these difficulties began to melt away when I started riding on the tractor with Larry. They disappeared completely with the approach of my thirteenth birthday. That was when I started driving the tractor.

Baling hay was my first driving job. With someone loading the bales on the wagon, I was never alone. The next spring, when I had gained enough driving skill, I worked the fields unaccompanied. After school, I disked and cultivated, preparing the seed bed, while the men did the barn chores.

As my familiarity with the tractor increased, my caution decreased. Being young, feeling indestructible, and not appreciating the dangers of operating heavy equipment, I took foolish chances. To this day, whenever my brothers and I reminisce, we are amazed we lived to graduate from high school. To survive growing up on the farm, a person needs a great deal of common sense with an adequate leavening of luck. We lacked the common sense, so we depended on luck.

My first near-accident occurred when I was preparing the corn ground for planting. In a hurry to start the job, I throttled up the tractor and popped the clutch.

"Holy shit!" I thought. "The front wheels are lifting! What can I do? They're still going up. What the hell? Pull the clutch. All right!"

The front wheels hit the ground with a thud. This time, I gently engaged the clutch, not wanting to repeat the near-accident. I escaped death that time but learned nothing from the experience.

From the way we acted while baling hay, it was obvious that we had learned nothing from our previous mistakes. Sometimes, if Larry was loading the bales, he gave me a "gotcha" surprise. He ran from the wagon and over the bales in the chute, then ended up standing on the plunger shield. Leaning forward, he grabbed the tractor seat and fender, putting a foot on the tractor platform. He then grabbed me, shouting, "Gotcha!" Concentrating on driving, expecting nothing, I almost fell off the seat in shock. One sudden jerk of the steering wheel could have caused Larry to slip, falling onto the power takeoff and into the baler pickups. Death or serious injury would have been the result.

Late one Friday afternoon, while baling, I danced with death.

"John, I'll clear the bales off the chute," Frank said. "You can drive around and bale all the broken bales. I'll hitch up the wagons. I want to get this job done, get home, and get cleaned up. I've got a date tonight."

"Okay, Frank. I won't drop any of the bales. I'll meet you here when the chute is full. I want to get home and watch TV."

I thought, "If I start baling as I go up the hill, it'll save time. Engage the PTO. You're almost at the broken bale. Shit, the baler's gonna plug. Hit the clutch. That will let the baler clear the hay. Oh my God, I'm rolling backwards! Engage the clutch! Get the tractor going forward! Forget about the baler plugging. Holy shit, the front wheels are going up. Clutch in, clutch out—either way, a disaster. I can't do a damn thing except pray. If the wheels continue lifting, I'm gonna be crushed. Please, God, put the wheels back on the ground."

Gradually, after what felt like an eternity, the front wheels hit the ground. The rear wheels dug in, moving the tractor forward. I was not going to die that day.

Returning to the wagon, Frank asked, "What's the problem? You look pale. Good thing you're not going out tonight. Are you getting sick?"

The stupidest, most frightening near-accident took place when Larry and I were on the road returning from the field. Speeding down the hill on the final approach to home, Larry, having a faster tractor, began to overtake me.

When our tractors were wheel to wheel, a little voice in my head said, "John, you're not going to let Larry beat you. James Bond wouldn't let the bad guys speed past him. He would give them a little bump. It worked for James Bond, and it'll work for you. Just ease over, touch tires, and Larry will back off."

The voice changed. "Oh my God! Larry's rear tire is lifting. His tractor tire caught on my rim. He's gonna flip. Slow down! Let him pass!"

When we reached home, I knew I was in for it.

"You stupid ass! What were you trying to do? You almost killed me," Larry said.

"You tried to pass me. I did what James Bond would do if someone tried to pass him."

"What a stupid reason. You'd better hope Dad doesn't notice the cut in the tire."

My tractor-driving career was ending, but not because of my foolish antics. Larry was buying the farm, and we were moving.

Also, it was becoming more difficult for me to differentiate windrows of straw or hay from the surroundings. I could no longer easily discriminate between the subtle hues. However, my entrance into high school made accepting the end of my tractor-driving career much easier. Now there would be new challenges for me to meet.

7
Drugs

We grew up constantly exposed to alcohol. My stepfather, Frank, had made 160 gallons of hard cider and 20 gallons of wine. It was not difficult to sneak a bottle of cider out of the basement. At weddings, if you were tall enough to see over the bar, you were old enough to drink. Wine, cider, or homemade beer were usually the first drinks offered to guests. Drinking bore no social stigma unless you neglected your family.

As I grew older and started to attend high school, acceptance by my peers was of paramount importance. Being a paraplegic, I went out of my way to gain their acceptance. This led me to the school's outdoor smoking area, where much of the daily socializing took place. Morning, noon, and after school, kids gathered in the smoking area whether they smoked or not. It didn't take long before I was hooked on tobacco. Adults said it was harmful, but I didn't care as long as I was part of the group.

The following summer, while driving around, my close friend John pulled out a joint, saying, "Spark this up. I grew this."

After a few puffs, he asked, "Do you feel high? What do you think? How do you like it?"

I didn't know what to say. I mumbled something about being high, but truthfully, I didn't feel any different. On another occasion, I tried some hashish in a pipe with the same lack of result. My introduction to cannabis and its products was a flop. I didn't understand why there was all the fuss. Booze gave me a better buzz.

One sunny afternoon while we were playing Monopoly, my friend John asked, "Do you want to smoke some black hash?"

"Sounds great!" my brother Frank exclaimed.

"Sure," I uncertainly chorused. "I hope I feel something this time," I muttered to myself.

"Here. Take a hit of this," Frank said, passing me the pipe.

For the next few minutes, there was very little conversation as the pipe made its way around the circle. We were too busy drawing on the pipe, holding the smoke in, letting it out, and catching our breath before taking another haul off the pipe.

This time, something happened.

The sun streaming through the large living room window became brighter. The yellow light appeared to glow. I felt surrounded by a cloud-like haze. I could see every tiny dust mote dancing in the golden light. A feeling of wellbeing infused me. The world was a cheerier place. I felt light, free, unencumbered.

Maintaining interest in the game became difficult. With every throw of the dice, we couldn't stop laughing. Soon mirth took over and the game degenerated to the point where we could no longer carry on.

Back in high school for the second year, it was not long before I joined others sneaking off school property and making our way to the power dam. Some drank, but like me, most of us smoked hashish or marijuana. I experimented with both the leaf-green marijuana buds and the black, tar-like hashish.

High school turned out to be a cornucopia of drugs. Having become accustomed to alcohol, tobacco, and cannabis, I searched for a greater thrill

"How much for the acid?" I asked.

"Two dollars. It doesn't look like much, but when you do it, cut it in half. Two trips for the price of one."

"What do they call it?"

"Double-barreled sunshine. Twice the sunshine for two bucks."

Reaching home, I found the house empty.

"Mom and Frank must be in town," I said to myself. "Perfect time to do the acid. Be careful with the tinfoil. You don't want to drop anything. What the hell? This orange pellet is smaller than a rice grain! It doesn't look like much, but I'm not going to take any chances. I'll listen to Dianne and only do half. This is so small, it's difficult to cut. I wonder how long before I feel the effects? I'll just lie on the bed with the lights out until something happens."

Listening to some music on my tape recorder, I anxiously waited for something to happen. Slowly, a feeling of lightness crept over me. I felt like a helium-filled balloon, ready to float away. Running my fingers along the bedspread, I felt at one with the blanket; I was becoming a part of the weave. It was not long before the full impact of the drug hit me.

"Wow! Look at all the colors exploding by the furnace pipe. There are more radiant colors than the fireworks display on Canada Day. Reds, oranges, yellows, and blues shooting up the pipe, looking like a fountain of dazzlingly colored water. I've never seen a light show like this, and it's all mine. I can lie back, being entertained forever. No, I can't!"

My mother was calling me.

"I'm in my bedroom," I answered.

"I'm putting the groceries away. Supper will be in half an hour."

"I'd better pull myself together," I told myself. "This acid is nothing like marijuana. Once the trip starts, there's no getting off."

"I hear you, Mom. I'm on my way."

"Supper is the last thing I want," I thought. "What I do want is to lie here and watch the light show, but I'd better get out there, or Mom will wonder what's wrong with me."

"Hi, Mom, Frank. How was Walkerton?"

"Busy," Mom replied. "How was school? Are you doing anything this weekend?"

"School was the same as always. Nothing special. Since it's Friday, Mike and John may come back later to play cards."

"Eat your supper. When you clean your plate, I have a surprise for you. I bought your favourite dessert, honey-glazed donuts."

"You're going to have a difficult time choking down the beans, corn, ham, and potatoes on your plate, John," I whispered to myself. "Everything tastes like sand. I need lots of milk to wash down supper."

"Thanks, Mom. You shouldn't have. You're too good to me."

"Oh, no," I thought. "More to eat. Just what I don't want."

"We all enjoy them," Mom commented. "Here, have one."

"Thanks, Mom. It tastes great."

I felt the honey oozing from the squishy donut when I squeezed it. It tasted like cardboard. I told myself to just eat it and get the meal over with.

After supper, I got lucky. Mom and Frank retired to the living room to watch television, leaving me to wash the dishes. Usually, I resented this dreary task. Not this time! This time was fun.

"Look at how the soap bubbles shimmer while changing color," I thought. "Reds, oranges, yellows, greens, blues, and violets—all the colors of the rainbow. Whenever I stir the water, the bubbles pop and dance, making a new picture. I could make magnificent works of art, swirling the colored bubbles all evening. I'd better not, though. Mom will start to wonder why I'm taking so long to do a job I hate."

Just as I dragged myself away from the vibrantly colored dishwater, a couple of friends arrived. They had walked from Chepstow for our Friday night card game. And what a game it was. It was like none I had ever participated in before.

"I can do no wrong," I thought. "I need an ace, I draw an ace. I have 20 showing for Black Jack. I feel guilty winning all the time. If I draw another card, maybe I'll go bust."

I didn't go bust. I drew the only card that made me a winner.

It was difficult concentrating on the game with the cards pulsating, appearing to breathe. The colors on the face cards seemed to sparkle with a florescent glow as the cards melted and solidified in my hand. It was the luckiest game of cards I had ever played.

Later, while watching the color TV, I recalled that we only had a black and white set.

After a while, I decided to try to get some sleep. No luck. It was 2:00, then 3:00 in the morning, and I was still wide awake. LSD does not relinquish its hold easily. Finally, I nodded off to the sound of trilling birds.

I totally enjoyed the hallucinatory experience brought about by the LSD. I had experienced the cards, water, and stovepipe in a completely new manner. I moved from a simple recognition of their surface qualities to a deeper understanding of their elemental constituents. This positive experience encouraged me to go on another acid trip.

Like the previous LSD trip, I thoroughly enjoyed the phantasms and hallucinations the LSD had in store for me.

When I used LSD later in life, I never gained insights or experienced any hallucinations like in the past. What people sold as LSD was not. Today, if I could find true LSD, I would try it again, hoping to connect with and gain insights into a greater spiritual world.

With real LSD difficult to find, my drugs of choice became tobacco, alcohol, and marijuana. Tobacco and alcohol were the most common drugs used by my peer group. I smoked cigarettes daily. Binge drinking and the consumption of marijuana took place on the weekends. Health was of no concern. It was all about experimenting and proving your manhood.

The guys with girlfriends tended to use drugs less. Women didn't want their dates inebriated. Having girlfriends, those boys didn't have to constantly prove their manhood by binge drinking and smoking. Being left out of the dating game made me feel unwanted. I felt that I was missing an important part of life. This caused me to increase my drug use as I tried to bury my sadness.

Since I couldn't grow the marijuana I used, I needed to buy it. Unlike my friends, because of my paralysis, I couldn't get a summer job to earn money. I tried different businesses, but they all wanted people with two working legs. Mom gave me an allowance, but that was not the same as earning my own money. It made me feel like a child. I wanted to be a man, dependent on no one for handouts.

I started to sell marijuana and hashish, but only to friends. I made enough to get the small amount I smoked and maybe buy a pitcher of beer when I was out with the boys. It never crossed my mind to gain new customers by talking nonsmokers into using. I knew that having to sell drugs was temporary. Later in life, when I had a profession, I would be able to buy the marijuana.

Later in my life, some life-altering circumstances arose that caused me to increase my drinking. Fortunately, this was temporary, lasting until I passed over the rough spots. On the day of my mother's funeral, I felt her spirit infuse me with the strength to quit smoking cigarettes. I never smoked again after that.

However, using marijuana is a practice I've continued for my entire life, although I ceased smoking cannabis shortly after I quit cigarettes. Today, I eat the marijuana in brownies and soups. It has become another indispensable drug I use daily to help with my breathing and pain. When stress causes my airways to close, the marijuana helps relieve the anxiety, allowing the airways to open. Mitigating my pain from the polio-caused scoliosis and helping me sleep are two more uses I've found for marijuana.

8
Rite of Passage

In rural Ontario, the long distances made driving a necessity. Whether going three kilometers (1.8 miles) to school or six kilometers to the home of a friend or relative, we needed a vehicle to traverse the dusty gravel side roads. These distances were too far for me to push the wheelchair or walk with crutches and braces. The snows of winter only made the distances seem longer. Short cuts through the fields, used by the other children, were unavailable to me, as the tall hay and the rough farm lanes curtailed the maneuverability of the wheelchair. I was not free to go where or when I wanted. Mom or Frank always had to drive me if I wanted to leave the farm.

With the start of high school, my circle of friends increased, making a ride more important. My new friends were from Walkerton, 15 kilometers away. I definitely needed transportation if I wanted to visit them.

"Hey, mom! Can I stay overnight at John's place? After school on Friday, I could go with him to his house instead of coming home on the bus. You could pick me up on Saturday after you finish the weekly shopping."

"I'm not sure. Did he ask his mother?"

"Yes, Mom. If you want, you can phone and ask."

"I might just do that. I haven't spoken to her for a while. Yes, you can go, and I'll pick you up on Saturday. Be ready."

Even though I got to visit in town, my teenage pride was offended by having my mother pick me up. I was impatient, waiting to get my driver's license. I hoped to restore some of the freedom robbed by the polio when I gained my driving permit.

I knew there would be no problem obtaining the driver's license when Mom finally allowed me to apply. My years of driving a tractor gave me all the confidence I thought I needed, although at times I had behaved less than responsibly. I hoped Mom didn't know about these lapses in judgement.

With the approach of the magic age of 16, I started pestering mom to allow me to get a learner's permit.

"Mom, I'm almost 16. It's time for me to get my license. If I had the license, you wouldn't have to drive me to visit friends. I could go to a show or on a date. If Anne had to go somewhere, I could drive her instead of you. I can't go anywhere I want because every place is too far away for me to push the wheelchair. I need the license to shake off the restrictions polio put on me. Come on, Mom. All the guys get their licenses at 16."

"That may be, Johnny, but you're not just one of the guys," she said. Sitting me down, she continued, "Because of your paralysis, the car will have to be fitted with hand controls. You drove tractors, but the hand controls on the car are much different. You don't deal with traffic when driving in the field. When driving on the road, 15 miles an hour is your maximum speed. I want you older, more responsible, before you obtain a permit to drive. When you turn 18, we'll enroll you in the driver–training course at high school and get the hand controls installed in the car. Then you can get your learner's permit."

Argument was useless. I would just have to accept that two more years had to pass before I could try for my driver's permit. Confident that I would obtain the precious permit at 18, I didn't worry about delaying this rite of passage for a couple more years.

For the next two years, if I wanted to be independently mobile, my thumb, crutches, and braces were the only things I could use. So that's exactly what I did. Sticking out my thumb, I started hitchhiking to Walkerton to hang out with my friends. I don't know if it was pity or trust, but I seldom waited long for a ride. Either way, I appreciated a speedy ride whenever rain or sleet fell. With my thumb extended in the universal sign for a ride, I was able to retrieve some of the freedom lost due to the polio. I wasn't going to allow the paralysis to get the better of me.

The one thing I wanted to do the most was date, but hitchhiking wouldn't help me there.

For the teenage male, dating is almost as important as driving. First, the young man gets his license. Then he hopes to convince a young woman to go on a date. Hitchhiking to a date would be embarrassing. I needed a license and car before I asked a girl out on a date. Double dating was a possibility, but none of my friends showed any interest in that. Another thing hampering my dating prospects was the reluctance on the part of women to ask men out on dates. A few more years would pass before women felt liberated enough to ask men out.

While I waited, I thought of little else besides driving. With only six months of the two years left, I started counting down the days. Finally, September 1973 arrived! I could barely contain my joy and excitement as the licensing process was about to begin. Finally, it was time to bring my dreams to fruition.

Mom purchased the hand controls needed to make the brake pedal, gas pedal, and light dimmer switch accessible. The automotive shop teacher consented to installing and calibrating the hand controls. While the car was being prepared, I started the driver training course offered by the high school.

With the end of the course quickly approaching, it was time for me to take the driver's test to obtain a learner's permit. I needed the permit so our instructor could take me out for lessons.

A couple of days after the car returned with the hand controls installed, I arrived from school to find no one home. Mom must have taken Frank to his doctor's appointment. That's when the idea hit me.

"Gunner stashed some weed on a fence line about a mile down the road," I said in my head. "You could use the wheelchair to go pick up the weed. On the other hand, since no one is home and the car has the hand controls, you could drive there. Whatever you do, you'd better be quick. You don't want the folks or neighbors to catch you driving around, or you'll be in for it."

Without a second thought, I leaped into the car, then backed out of the parking spot and into the lane. There were no neighbors' cars on the road, so I had clear driving. Reaching the lane to the field, I parked the car, ensuring it was invisible to anyone traveling on the road. Crutching to the rail fence, I grabbed the toolbox full of herb.

Quick as a bunny, I jumped into the car and made a beeline for home.

Back home, my head was abuzz with the excitement of driving a car for the first time.

"Wow!" I thought. "You really drove the car by yourself! You're now king of the road, free to leap into a car and fly like a bird wherever you want. You've been dreaming of this ever since the polio robbed you of your mobility."

Because of my woolgathering, the folks found me still sitting in the car when they returned.

"Hi, Mom, Frank," I said. "How was town? I was just getting the feel of the car and the new hand controls. I can hardly wait to start driving."

"I hope that's all you were doing. You'd better not drive without a license. You're not insured, so you'll wait until you can legally drive the car."

"Yes, Mom."

I was elated. At last I would be going to the driver examination center and would leave with a learner's permit. The freedom I had looked forward to for years was finally within my grasp. I would no longer be dependent on others to get around. Dating would now be an option. I was on Cloud Nine!

There were three steps to pass before I received a learner's permit. I aced the 20 multiple-choice questions. The next step in the testing process was sign recognition. They flashed different colored and shaped road signs on the screen for me to identify. Again, no problem. The last, but what would turn out to be the most important part of the examination, was determining my field of vision. With the test completed, my heart sank when I saw the examiner's somber countenance.

Handing me a form, he commiserated with me. "I'm so sorry, Mr. Cronin. The numbers I get for your field of vision are not adequate for me to issue a learner's permit. However, the equipment I use is crude. Take this form to your optometrist and have him fill it out. When he's determined that your field of vision is wide enough and has filled out the form, you can bring it back, and I'll issue the permit. Looking forward to seeing you shortly. Have a good day."

My desolation was obvious to everyone, but reining in my emotions, I put on a brave face.

"This is just a minor bump in the road to my license and freedom," I thought. "I have faith. I know the optometrist can remedy any problems with my sight, and I'll be able to get my license."

On the ride home, the pestering started.

"Mom, I need the optometrist appointment right away. I can't take the suspense. I'm anxious. When we get home, you could phone and get me an appointment for tomorrow."

"Sorry, John. By the time we get home, the office will be closed. I'll phone tomorrow, but I can't promise that you'll get an appointment the next day. I'll try my best, though."

"Thanks, Mom. You're the greatest. I'm still a little worried, though. I've always needed really thick glasses. Do you think there'll be problems when I see the optometrist?"

"I don't know. I only know what they tell me."

The wait was nerve-wracking. During the day, when around family and friends, I was confident about obtaining my license. But at night, I couldn't sleep, fretting about my eyesight. In the deepest, darkest part of the night, fear overwhelmed me. The question reverberated in my head: "Will my eyes fail me in the crunch?"

Finally, the day arrived. Nervous as a cat in a dog pound, I was unable to think clearly. I needed to gain control over the relentless chatter in my head if I wanted to do my best on the test.

I gave myself a pep talk. "John! Get hold of yourself. You won't accomplish anything shaking like a leaf in a windstorm. The visit to the optometrist is only a formality. Your eyesight won't let you down. Although all your dreams for the future ride on this single eye test, you will remain calm and succeed. You will sit in the chair and look at the screen. The optometrist will fill out the form and send it to the examination center. You will then be the proud owner of a learner's permit. Yes! You can do it!"

Pumped up, I was ready for the test. I knew there was no problem.

But there was a problem, a very big one.

With empathy in his voice, the optometrist delivered the verdict. "I'm very sorry, John. Your field of vision is too narrow to fulfill the requirements for a learner's permit. I can arrange an appointment with an ophthalmologist in Owen Sound, but there's nothing more I can do for you. Here's the form. The ophthalmologist may help."

However, his voice was not reassuring. It sounded more like a judge pronouncing sentence on a condemned man, and that was exactly how I felt. My dreams came crashing to an end, betrayed by my Judas eyes.

Stoically, I marched from the office. Once in the car, however, I broke down, blubbering like a baby. Tears poured from my eyes and rolled down my cheeks. Sobs wracked my body. I tried regaining my self-control, but I couldn't stop shaking. It felt like there was a cold, hard rock where my heart had been. Hiccups possessed me, leaving me unable to speak clearly.

Taking a couple of deep breaths, I regained some control, allowing me to gasp out, "My life is ruined. I can't drive. I can't go out on dates. Everything I hoped for is gone. What's the use in living?"

Mom wiped my eyes and nose. She hugged me and whispered, "Don't talk like that. There's always something to live for. The ophthalmologist will be able to help you. Don't give up hope. You've always been a survivor. You survived the polio and learned how to live with the problems from it. No matter what problems you faced, you always adapted. You'll bounce back from this one." Giving me an extra tight hug, she murmured, "No matter what happens, I'll always be here for you, John."

That night, once again, the chatter in my head didn't let me sleep. "You can't drive. You can't date. Your life is in ruins." Repeatedly, the mantra ran through my head.

Soon the tears started to flow, and I silently sobbed into my pillow. Would the pain ever end? Not for another week, when the appointment with the ophthalmologist finally arrived.

The hour's ride to the ophthalmologist passed in relative silence. Mom said very little, only remarking on the weather. She didn't try to build up my hopes. We would arrive at the office, and what would be, would be.

I was a bundle of nerves. This was it. This cast of the dice would determine my future.

At the office, I put all the noise in my head to rest, concentrating on the task before me. Maybe, just maybe, something that only the ophthalmologist knew could save my dream. I was riding an emotional rollercoaster of hope and disappointment.

Before starting the examination, I did some deep breathing exercises, hoping to gain control over my nerves and thoughts. Having somewhat settled, I strove with every fiber of my being to maximize my field of vision.

"Lean forward and place your chin in the rest," the doctor told me. "That's correct. Stare straight ahead at the white dot in the center of the black screen. I will then use a pointer to slide a white dot over the black screen, moving the dot from the periphery to the center of the screen. Tell me when you can see the dot. Are you ready?"

"Yes."

For the next five minutes, I stared intently at the screen, piping up the instant I perceived the dot. I had a seemingly simple task, but still, the sweat trickled under my arms and down my back. Finally, the ordeal concluded.

"I am sorry, Mr. Cronin, but your field of vision is not adequate for a driver's license in Ontario. The cause of your restricted field of vision is a disease called RP, or retinitis pigmentosa. A genetic flaw causes it. There's nothing I can do to help you regain your field of vision. The damage is permanent. I wish I could help you."

Reaching the car, I could no longer hold back my tears as I sobbed out, "There's no more hope. This was my final chance for a license. Everything I dreamed of just went up in smoke. The freedom I hoped for is no longer possible. "

"That's not true," Mom stated, wiping tears from my eyes and cheeks. "Everything looks bleak today, but things will work out. Your life hasn't changed. Only your expectations have."

"But those were everything, Mom. I expected to be able to drive to visit friends and go on dates. Now all that's gone forever! Life isn't worth living."

"Life isn't over for you, John. The polio may have taken away your ability to walk, but you never quit trying. Your life is just veering off in a direction you didn't expect. Next year, you'll attend university. Think of the many new experiences you'll enjoy while there. With all the sidewalks, it'll be easy for you to negotiate the campus with the wheelchair. Dating is also a possibility when you go to university. Staying in residence means you could take a girl on a date without needing a car. You won't gain all the freedom the polio took from you, but you'll gain a great deal. Promise me you won't give up. You have a great future. You've always done well in school. Later on, you can get a well-paying job and hire a driver. You can overcome anything, John! All you have to do is believe in yourself. Look to the future! The past is past."

With one last sniffle, I pulled myself together. "You're right, Mom. I have no choice. I can either get on with life and make the best of it or lie down and die. I've never been a quitter, and I won't give up now. Don't worry. I mean what I said. I promise to never take the easy way out."

Note

For more information on the disease of retinitis pigmentosa, check the following website:

https://en.wikipedia.org/wiki/Retinitis_pigmentosa

9
Snowmobiling

Depression hung over me like a storm cloud after my failure to obtain a driver's license. The loss tainted everything I thought and did. I saw no future.

"Mom, I need a ride to Glen's house."

"I'm busy. Ask your sister."

"Anne, drive me to Glen's house."

"No. I have a few things I need to do."

"You have to take me. Mom told you to."

"No, she told you to ask me."

"You're just being mean because you have a license and I can't get one. If you were a nice sister, you would drive me."

"Maybe if you were a nicer brother, I would drive you."

"Mom, Anne won't drive me. Make her."

"I will not. Just because you're angry about not getting a license, that doesn't give you the right to take it out on your sister. She's not your slave. Grow up and behave."

"I'm sorry, Anne. I'm jealous of you. You have a driver's license, and I'll never have one."

In an attempt to lift my spirits, Mom bought a snowmobile

for Anne and me, although I was the main user. Waiting for the snow to arrive, I sometimes sat on the machine after school, pretending I was flying over the endless fields of virgin white snow. Finally, the snow did arrive.

With snowmobile suit on and helmet and goggles in place, I was ready for adventure. With the machine full of gas and oil and my crutches strapped to the running boards, I yanked the pull cord. The snowmobile barked to life. Straddling the seat, I nudged the throttle, and the machine leapt forward like a cat pouncing on a mouse.

My newfound independence had me intoxicated as I flew over the fields of pristine snow. I had never imagined I could experience this degree of autonomy. The restrictions polio imposed on me disappeared. There were miles of untouched snow and evergreen forests waiting for me to explore.

Until I grew accustomed to handling the snowmobile, I didn't venture far from home. Still, there were plenty of things to investigate. I accessed snowy fields and bush trails I had never travelled before. At times, when in a particularly picturesque locale, I turned off the machine and listened to the silence while drinking in the beauty of a still, sunny winter afternoon. If I remained still and silent long enough, the birds sang for my private joy. At other times, rabbits, weasels, and coyotes made an appearance. I could never have indulged in this rapport with nature without the snowmobile to take me to these isolated locations.

During the day, the snowmobile was my magic carpet. However, my low vision created new problems when driving after dusk. If I didn't pay attention to the time of day, the light would wane, and I would end up driving when I shouldn't have.

One afternoon I overstayed a visit to a friend. By the time I left, the sun was sinking below the horizon, bathing the world in a dusky twilight. Because of the shadows cast by the low light, I didn't see the barbed wire strung between the maple trees bordering the field.

Before I met the fence line, a voice inside me yelled out, "Go slow! There were cattle in this field last year, so there must have been barbed wire strung between the trees. I can't see it. Oh shit, the windshield! What am I doing on the ground? Where are my helmet and scarf? There they are. Quick, put them on and get out of here."

The barbed wire had scraped over the windshield, dragging me off the snowmobile and pulling off my helmet and scarf. Thank God I was not going fast, or the wire would have ripped off my head, leaving me a headless corpse for searchers to find the next day.

At home, I easily avoided scrutiny because of all the company. First stop, the bathroom mirror.

Unwinding the gray and black plaid scarf, I softly exclaimed, "Wow! I have three ragged cuts over my Adam's apple. A little faster, and no more John. This is as close to death as I ever want to come. I'd better wear my turtleneck sweater until the cuts heal. If Mom sees them, I'll be grounded for life."

Another time, dusk caught me at the King Edward Hotel with some friends.

"I'd better get going," I said. "It's almost suppertime. I don't want to end up like Valena." She was a local woman who lived about two kilometers from the King Edward Hotel. Leaving the hotel late one stormy afternoon, she took a short cut and never made it home. They found her body the next spring.

"Right," one of my companions said. "The snow is getting heavier. If you don't want to end up like her, you'd better get moving. Do you need any help getting the Ski–Doo started?"

"No problem. I got it."

Starting up the machine, I noticed dark descending and snow starting to sift down. This was just like the night Valena had gone missing.

"Get that out of your head," I told myself.

I knew that pushing hard would get me home in five minutes. Telling the difference between the ditch and the road was a different matter. I passed the river and Larry's gate. Home was not much farther.

But everything looked white. Shit, I was in the steep-sided, deep ditch near Larry's gate.

Fear of turning over kept me from trying to regain the road. Riding the ditch to the bottom, I hoped I could drive out. I kept the throttle wide open to prevent the machine from bogging down in all the loose powder. Finding Larry's lane, I knew I was almost home free. All I needed to do was to get on the road and drive straight home. I made sure to drive slowly, not wanting to end up in another ditch. Thank God, I made it.

Another near miss. I would have to be more careful, but I couldn't stop sledding. I couldn't relinquish the freedom the snowmobile gave me.

I drove the snowmobile to school over the trails and back roads. I visited friends in Paisley. Solitary excursions into the wilderness and trail rides with the local snowmobile club became pastimes I relished.

After one year of enjoying the freedom provided by the snowmobile, it was time to start university. When I made it to campus, I knew that wheeling around was possible, as it had been in Teeswater, but the personal liberty I had experienced while driving the snowmobile for the past two years remained unequaled.

To this day, looking back, I still yearn for the choices the snowmobile provided me. However, I'm also thankful that my inferior vision didn't cause me to incur any injuries while riding.

10
University

"This is it. At last I have my own place to live. I'm no longer subject to Mom's rules. I'm free to go and come and have visitors whenever I want."

These were the thoughts running through my head as Mom helped me move my stereo, clothes, and favourite patchwork quilt to my new residence. I was commencing my post-secondary education at the University of Waterloo.

With everything unpacked, it was time for Mom to head home. As she departed, she gave me a big hug and kiss, saying, "Be good. Work hard at all your classes. Remember, you need a job that takes brains. I love you. We'll miss you."

"Don't worry, Mom. I'll work hard. I can get a ride with Frank when he heads home. We'll be home at least once a month."

With that, Mom departed, leaving me to exercise my newfound freedom.

Hungry and wanting to get oriented, I sought out the cafeteria. When I saw the cornucopia of foods available, I was amazed. The entrees, side dishes, desserts, and drinks were endless. At home, I got one choice, and if I didn't like it, too bad.

With one of the kitchen staff carrying my loaded tray, I looked for a table with friendly faces. Seeing my indecision, a don from another house called out, "Over here. Join us. I'm Bill Jackson. I'm the don of West 1. These guys are in my house."

"Hello. I'm John, from South 1. None of the other students on my floor have arrived yet. Makes for a lonely life."

"This is frosh week. Only first-year students come this early. Everyone else will arrive by next week, when classes start."

"I'm bored over there. What can I do for excitement?"

"The Campus Center is where students usually go for entertainment. It has a video games room, food services, and a pub."

"The pub sounds right up my alley."

With a full stomach, it was time to start exploring.

Wheeling along the paved sidewalks on my way to the pub, my brain was abuzz with all the possibilities now available to me.

"John," I told myself, "with these paved sidewalks all over campus, you could go wherever and whenever you want in the wheelchair. You no longer have to beg for a ride, waiting for someone to pick you up. This is the first time you've gone to a pub alone. You're much freer than you ever were at home."

I had smooth wheeling all the way to the Campus Center. There was no problem entering the building, as there were no steps hindering my entrance.

But what was this? I had to get down six steps to the pub. I didn't see any ramp. So much for all the freedom I thought I had. I would have to beg for some help. It was humiliating, but there was no way around it if I wanted a beer.

"Hello! Yes, you, working security at the door. I need you to help me bump the wheelchair down the steps."

"I'm not strong enough," the woman said. "I'll get one of the men to help you down."

While she stamped my hand, I asked, "Why did you think you couldn't help me down the steps? My mother and sister do it. This is the 1970s. Women are liberated. If women think they can't do the job, then there always has to be a man present for door security."

"You'll have to take that up with the student council," she answered. She was obviously none too pleased.

With the approach of the witching hour, I quaffed the last sips of beer and departed for my new home. Arriving at my room, I found a pizza flyer from a student-run pizza shop, which was located in the residence building. Picking up the phone, I did something I never could do before.

"Hello. Yes. I would like to order a small pizza with ham, pepperoni, extra cheese, and hot peppers. I'll be in the lounge."

Hanging up the phone, I moved to the lounge and turned on the television.

"Right on," I slurred. "The television is in color. And it's connected to cable. I can't believe my luck. Color and cable. Beats the hell out of black and white with two channels. You've hit the big time, John. How about sparking up a joint? By the time the pizza arrives, you'll have the munchies."

"Did you order a small pizza?" the pizza delivery woman inquired.

"You've got the right guy."

Nose twitching like a rabbit's, she asked, "What do I smell? It doesn't smell like pizza."

"It certainly does not. Do you want a haul off the joint?"

"Sure."

"Here, finish this one. I just rolled another. Take it as a tip."

Waking the next morning with a fuzzy head, I was still the only student in South 1. After lunch, it was time to investigate the campus. With my class schedule and a map in hand, I started exploring.

Shooting along the paved paths, I realized, "These paths don't have expansion joints. That's why the ride is so smooth. The curb cut-outs make it easy to cross the road. This is so much nicer than back home."

Entering Hagey Hall, I thought, "This is where most of my classes will take place. I might as well go up to the third floor and find the classrooms. Yes, there's the elevator. No problem getting around so far. I'm going to love it here."

Now that I knew where the philosophy and political science classes were, it was time to find my accounting class. The schedule indicated that the class would be held in the Engineering 1 building, but when I entered the building, there were steps and no ramp. How could I get to class?

"Sir, could you help me?"

"I'd be happy to. What can I do for you?"

"How do I get to the engineering lecture hall without going down steps?"

Looking into space as if studying a map, he stated, "You can, but it's a convoluted route. Go into Engineering Two. You'll find a freight elevator. Go down one floor. When you come out, turn to your left and follow the hall to the end. You'll find a few steps, but there's a ramp to your left. The lecture hall is on your right."

"Thanks a lot. I'm glad I only have this class once a week."

On another day, I ventured out to the bank. I needed to open an account so I could cash my student loan cheque. Arriving at the Campus Center, once again I faced steps if I wanted to go to the bank. Asking at the student information desk was useless. They knew nothing. Someone suggested talking with someone from maintenance.

Finding a worker in a green maintenance uniform, I inquired, "Sir, is there any way to get to the bank without using steps?"

Scratching his head, he said, "Go outside the way you came in. Head to the ring road. On your right, you'll see a lane leading to a loading dock in the basement of the Campus Center. There's a short, steep ramp up to the dock. Pull open the door, wheel down the hall, and you'll find the bank and record store. It's a heavy door. You may need help."

I was finding out that the accessibility of the campus didn't live up to the administration's billing. The paved paths and curb cut-outs were there to make biking more enjoyable. The use of wheelchairs had apparently never crossed their mind when laying out the campus. If they wanted to portray this campus as wheelchair accessible, they needed to create a map with all the complicated wheelchair routes marked on it. If those in charge put together such a map, it would become obvious to them that the campus was not actually wheelchair accessible.

I endured all the inconveniences with no complaining to the newspaper or administration. They expected disabled people to muddle along as best they could. I learned not to expect society to spend money to make life easier for the disabled. We did not exist.

Wheeling to class in winter was difficult. The paths were usually plowed and salted, but any remaining slush accumulated on the wheels, soaking my mittens. At times like that, I appreciated a helping hand.

By the time I reached class, my hands would be numb from the cold. If I wanted to hold a pen, I had to wash my hands in hot water to thaw the joints. The tingling as the frost left the fingers was always painful. I also needed to wash off all the salt and sand that had accumulated while pushing the wheelchair.

With the residence hall filling up, it was time to meet the other students on my floor. After everyone's arrival, it became obvious that I had landed on the gimp floor. Half of us had medical problems such as blindness, using an artificial leg or wheelchair, or cystic fibrosis. There was a wheelchair-accessible bathroom, but only two of us used a wheelchair.

Why did they insist we all stay on the same floor? Those not using a wheelchair should have been able to stay in any residence, since they didn't need any special facilities. It all came down to the ignorance of the person in charge of housing. It seemed to me that he thought of all disabled people as one amorphous mass. He didn't recognize that individual problems needed individual treatment. Put us all on the gimp floor, and the problem disappears.

I enjoyed all my roommates' company, but Phil and I formed an especially close bond. We discussed everything. At times, we went for drives through the countryside, especially when the fall colors were at their most radiant. On occasion, we ended up at my parents' for supper. By the end of my first year, we were inseparable.

"I'm going to miss you next year, Phil, when you're a don in Village 2," I told him. "I won't be able to wheel next door for a visit like now. Coming to visit you in Village 2 is difficult because there's no path between the two residences."

"Well, young John, there's no reason you couldn't live in Village 2. The showers are not accessible, but there's a bathtub you could use. The toilet stalls are wheelchair friendly."

"So you think I could live in Village 2?"

"Yes. Next year, when I'm don there, I'll try to convince administration to change their policy. I don't see any reason why they would refuse."

"All right, sounds fantastic! I hope it comes true. I'm looking forward to more good times."

I'm glad to say that in the latter half of my second term, I broke the mold. I moved to South 1 residence in Village 2. After my precedent-setting move, they no longer segregated the disabled students.

Classes finally began with Accounting 101. Struggling with the freight elevator and various doors, at last I arrived at the class. The lecture hall was huge. All my other classes were small, taking place in the more intimate setting of regular classrooms.

Looking around, I thought, "Look at all the students taking this accounting course. There must be three hundred or more, and everyone wants to be an accountant. There'll be accountants counting accountants. I think I might change my major from accounting to political science and philosophy. Those will be excellent preparation for law."

On my next visit to my social worker, she asked, "How are you doing in your program? Accounting was a better choice for you than law. There are more jobs in accounting, and the program isn't as long."

"Social services may think accounting is a better choice for me," I told her, "but I saw enormous rooms full of people wanting to be accountants. I didn't see rooms full of people trying to be lawyers. I enjoy the philosophy and political science courses more than accounting. If I enjoy the subjects, I'll work hard, getting better grades."

"It's not all about what you enjoy, John. Too bad you didn't do better in accounting. Since you no longer want to take our advice, we will no longer pay your tuition or for your books.

However, you'll still receive the regular disability allowance. I'm sorry you won't follow our suggestions. Good luck with your studies."

"Your program is too strict," I said. "You must allow people to get the education they want and not base everything on job statistics. If students enjoy the subjects, they'll work extra hard."

(An important note here concerning finances: I was able to continue my education because I received loans and grants. I also worked for four terms as a teaching assistant.)

Because it was the gimp floor, we made it entertaining. In the evenings, those who had finished their homework gathered in the lounge, where we got to know our neighbors.

"Where is everyone from?" I asked.

"Toronto, Scarborough, Ottawa," were the chorused responses.

"Is there anyone from a farm or small town?" I inquired.

"I'm from Stratford, but it has about 15,000 people. I don't think that qualifies as a small town."

"You're not going to find farmers here," someone else said. "They go to the University of Guelph. It has a school of agriculture."

"With everyone else hailing from a good-sized town or the big city, I feel like a country bumpkin," I lamented. "I had to come to university in order to get cable TV or have a pizza delivered. I've always felt like I was on the outside looking in."

"Don't worry about that. You're here now, with all the amenities that go with civilization."

"John, can you get me a beer, please? Don't forget to put a check mark beside my name." The beer and pop pool was a great idea, as long as everyone was honest and marked down all their drinks.

"Does anyone want a hit off the joint?"

"I'll take one. With homework done, it's time to relax. Pass that over here!"

"I'm ready for bed. The beer and joints really whacked me out."

My time at university was not all drinking, smoking, and partying, although I did get the nickname Smoking John, or SJ. Schoolwork was my first priority. I learned from my peers to keep up with the work, no matter how easy it appeared. Those who ignored their work didn't return the next year.

I enjoyed all my courses except for Accounting 101. Unlike accounting, philosophy, political science, and economics were subjects where debate and questions were welcome. There were no absolute truths, only gray areas ripe for argument. I knew learning to think and assess arguments would help me prepare for law school.

"Having failed Accounting 101," I told myself, "I'll have to work harder to bring up my average when I return next year. This will be much easier because I'll enjoy the subjects. If I want to continue university, I can't afford another failure. I vow to do whatever I need to continue my education. My future depends on my brain, not my back."

11
Travel

Having had eight months of socializing and study, I dreaded the end of term. I saw a boring summer stretching out before me. Everything changed with a visit from my cousin John.

"How would you like to drive to California with me?" he asked. "I've always wanted to drive across America to the West Coast. With two weeks of vacation about to start, I thought this would be the perfect time to go. What do you think, John?"

"It sounds great! Count me in! You saved me from a dull summer."

"We can split the cost of gas and motels. The car had a tune-up a couple of weeks ago, so it should make it out and back."

"When do you want to leave?"

"My holidays start this coming Friday. If you can be ready, we can leave early Saturday."

"No problem. I'll be ready to go. I'm thrilled that you asked me to accompany you on your adventure!"

Thoughts of the trip excited me, making sleep impossible. Waking early on Saturday, I packed, ate breakfast, and waited for John. While I waited, my mind wandered back to previous journeys.

"Frank's cousin is getting married in Montreal," Mom told me. "Frank and I are talking about going. If we go, I want to take you to the three shrines in the province of Quebec. In the past, Jesus performed many miracles at these shrines. The only way to cure the effects of polio is through His intercession. Maybe He will look down upon you and bless you with a miracle."

"That sounds great, Mom. I've never been that far from home. I'm going to another province! Will we board the train in Cargill? Will it take us all the way to Montreal?"

"Yes to all your questions. We leave early in the morning, arriving at Montreal in the late afternoon."

The train trip was a fantastic experience for a young child of 10. Usually Mom dragged me out of bed in the morning, but not that day. I was wide-awake, dressed, and ready to board the train at 6 a.m.

"Look at the cars stopped at the crossing," I said, "waiting for us to pass. Everything looks so different from the train."

"That's right, John. The trains run along the backs of towns. You see the poorer parts of cities."

Later, I piped up, "Look at all the houses. I see skyscrapers. Everything is so big, and there are so many people!"

"Wait until we get to the train station."

"Wow, Mom, you're right. There must be thousands of people. I'm a little scared."

"Don't worry. I'll push you while we make our way to the next train."

On the second leg of our trip, we traveled from Toronto to Montreal. Again, the scenery consisted of back yards and alleys, but Lake Ontario and the Saint Lawrence River were a wonderful sight. When we arrived at Montreal, Uncle Tom and Aunt Mary met us.

The Sunday after the wedding, we attended a Mass at Saint Joseph's Oratory.

Pulling Mom's sleeve, I gestured toward my surroundings, whispering, "This church is huge. I smell incense."

"If you light a votive candle, accompany it with your prayers," she told me. "The incense will waft your petitions to Heaven. If it's Jesus' wish, He may grant your request."

When praying at the crypt holding the remains of Saint André Bessette, C.S.C., I pointed at the wall, saying, "Mom, look at all the crutches and braces hanging on the wall. Won't the children they belong to miss them? I would."

"No, John. They no longer need the braces and crutches. Jesus cured them. They left their crutches, braces, and artificial limbs behind for visitors to see. They are the proof of God's power and love."

The next stop on our pilgrimage to the holy sites of Quebec was the shrine of Cap-de-la-Madeleine located in the city of Three Rivers. I thought I had landed in another country.

"Mom, no one speaks English. All I hear is French. Why?"

"Quebec is mostly a French-speaking province. The majority of those speaking English live in Montreal."

Wheeling around the cathedral grounds, I visited the life-size Stations of the Cross with Mom, saying a prayer at each stop. With the church dedicated to Marian devotions, the parishioners recited the rosary 24 hours a day, every day of the year. This made it easy for us to join at any time.

As a child, I was more interested in the marble and stained glass windows of the basilica than prayer.

"Look at all the marble, Mom. The communion rail, floors,

statues—all use beautifully colored marbles. The reds, greens, and cream make everything look like a rainbow. See how the sun lights up the stained-glass windows! The way the bright colors paint the floors makes them beautiful. I feel like I'm driving through rainbows."

"All of the beauty and craftsmanship put into the cathedral is to glorify God, John. The cathedral celebrates the miracle He worked when the locals built the original church. Jesus froze the river, enabling the locals to haul logs across."

After a couple of days, we boarded a train heading to the shrine of Sainte-Anne-de-Beaupré. The natural scenery of the Laurentian Highlands in the fall is spectacular. White water cascaded off the Laurentian Highlands. Evergreens broke up the vivid reds, oranges, purples, and yellows of the maples, elms, oaks, and birch trees. This glorious setting is a fitting location for the basilica.

The majesty and grandeur of the basilica were unequaled by any of the previous churches. The interior of the basilica, like the cathedral of Cap-de-la-Madeleine, consisted of multi-hued marble everywhere. The most memorable feature of the basilica was the larger-than-life statue of Saint Anne. Her eyes seemed to follow me as I prayed for her to intercede with Jesus on my behalf.

While I was praying at the statue, a man came up, handed me a $20 bill, and asked, "Will you pray for me?"

"Thank you, sir. I will pray for your intentions. I hope God grants them."

Before departing for home, we attended one last Mass. There were six priests saying Mass, with 12 other men filling the role of altar boys. I never saw a Mass like that before or since.

"John, I'm sorry Jesus didn't grant you a miracle," my mother said. "We prayed, but our hopes did not come true. Jesus has other plans for you. He knows best."

Since John had not arrived, I continued reflecting on past excursions. Two summers earlier, I was lucky enough to join a five-week high school trip to Greece.

Climbing on the bus for the drive to the airport, thoughts of my adventure absorbed me.

"This is my first time flying," I thought. "I'm a little nervous. Toronto to Montreal is a short hop, but Montreal to Athens is over six hours. I'm also looking forward to getting to know the 22 others in our group."

On landing, culture shock hit me full force. Stepping from the plane, a bone-dry, furnace-like heat enveloped me. Wherever I looked in the arrival lounge, I saw soldiers toting machine pistols. I also saw a woman eating bread and cheese and drinking wine.

I spent the first week acclimatizing myself to the arid heat and becoming familiar with the university residence and the surrounding streets.

Before long, we started visiting the numerous historical and cultural sites.

When I was sitting in the wheelchair at Marathon, looking at the steps up the side of the barrow containing the ashes of the fallen Greek heroes, Mike asked, "Do you want us to lift you up the steps to look around? Matt and I can carry you up, and a couple of the girls can pull up the wheelchair. If you want to see how so few could hold so many back for so long, we can maneuver you over the scree to get you into the pass at Thermopylae. Once we get you and the wheelchair up the hill, you'll be on the headland of the island of Salamis. From there you can sit on your throne like Xerxes the Persian king did when he watched the Greeks defeat his fleet in a sea battle. To get you to the 13th-century Bronze Age Lion Gate guarding the acropolis of Mycenae, I'll have to carry you. The path is so narrow that Matt will have to fold the wheelchair to pull it up the hill."

I enjoyed visiting the ancient Athenian agora, or marketplace, as it was one of the few places I could wander without help.

The Athenian acropolis was a different story. I wanted to wheel around the Ionian pillars on the acropolis, so my friends had to pull me and the wheelchair up the marble steps. Once at the top, I could push myself around.

Reading history is consuming dry facts with no physical context to anchor them. Seeing and touching historical places and buildings and other artifacts put it into context for me, making remembering easy.

On other occasions, we attended plays at the Odeon of Herodes Atticus, which is a huge amphitheatre in Athens, and at the theatre located high on Mount Parnassus, overlooking the sanctuary of Delphi, where we saw plays written by Sophocles and Aristophanes. Before attending, we studied the plays. This made understanding the action much easier.

I was not accustomed to theatres like these. The stage was a minimal raised stone area, with very little scenery. The different masks worn by the actors were all that indicated the actor's role. The only concessions made to the modern theatre were the use of a loudspeaker system and lighting. The biggest surprise was sitting on stone benches.

Another aspect of ancient Greek life was religion. We visited the religious sanctuary of Delphi, dedicated to Apollo. When visiting Olympia, I remembered that the games and temple were religious sites dedicated to Zeus, father of the gods.

Exploring the Minoan Palace of Knossos on the island of Crete was only possible with the help of my friends.

"We can get you to the upper stories," they said, "but the lower sections were not designed for wheelchairs. You can hang out here beside these oleander bushes while we explore the bottom floors."

After a day of planes and buses, I finally returned to Walkerton, where I had started the journey.

Before climbing off the bus, I shook hands with Mike and Matt. "Thanks a lot, guys. Without your help getting the chair and me up and down steps and over rough ground, I would have missed so much. Your including me in everything really made my trip. Thanks for everything!"

For me, the trip was more than a catalogue of historical sites visited. It really opened my eyes. Different language, different food, different climate, different attitudes—they all gelled, giving me a new perspective on life. I realized that the Canadian way was not the only way to organize a society. Exposure to the Greek way of life gave me greater respect, acceptance, and tolerance for other cultures and people.

My daydreams ended when I heard John call out, "Are you ready? Time to go."

On the second day of our trip, as we drove over the bridge, I exclaimed, "So, this is the mighty Mississippi! The river is huge."

"I think people also call it the Big Muddy because of all the soil it washes away," John told me.

"I guess we're now in Iowa," I said. "This is where Radar O'Reilly, the character from MASH, came from."

Gazing through the car window as we drove through the

countryside, I couldn't keep from comparing what I saw to what I had left behind.

"This countryside is boring," I thought. "Flat, no trees, with a house, barn, and silo plunked down every few miles among the endless rows of corn. I wouldn't want to live here, especially at night, isolated among miles and miles of corn. When the rustling stalks sound like whispering voices, madness stalks the night."

Another day on the road found us driving into a radically different landscape.

"What a difference," I thought. "No more hot, dusty, dry cornfields. The air feels cooler and fresher. We must be climbing the foothills of the Rockies. I see Denver. At last we can rest after our 24-hour road trip."

Rested and refreshed, we were off to the Garden of the Gods in Colorado Springs. The wind-sculpted sandstone, conglomerates, and limestone come in hues of deep red, pink, and white. The landscape of jumbled red rocks reminded me of the settings for the Road Runner cartoons.

The next day, our journey took us through Rocky Mountain National Park.

"John, look," I said. "We left Denver in the rain. Now it's bright and sunny, with not a cloud in the sky. The bicyclists we just passed must have a great deal of strength and stamina to pedal up the mountain, especially with their large backpacks. It must be cold for them to have all that winter gear on. I know temperature drops with altitude, but it feels warm in the car."

"Open the window and check the temperature," John suggested.

I cracked the window and cold air poured in—but not for long.

At about 12,000 feet, we crossed the Great Divide, where rivers separate, flowing east or west. Coming down the west side of the mountains, I exclaimed, "What a spectacular sight! I can see forever. Everything looks like a world in miniature. Trees, rivers, rocks, and towns all spread out before us. I feel like a god looking over his domain."

Next stop, Salt Lake City.

"John, this is the cleanest city I've ever been in. The Mormons are as busy as bees keeping the place clean. That must be why we see bees carved all about the Temple."

The Salt Lake Temple is a magnificent building, with features like perfect acoustics. However, having read about rocket cars setting land speed records on the Bonneville Salt Flats, the Temple became less interesting to me.

Arriving at the interpretive center at the Salt Flats, I grumbled, "Is this all there is? One lonely, dilapidated building with a few pictures of rocket cars. No models, no door, nothing permanent. What a disappointment! Nothing but miles of hardpan salt, with saturated brine below. I'm glad to get out of that hell hole."

As day waned, we found ourselves climbing into the Sierra Nevada. The cool, clear mountain air was a welcome relief after the hot Nevada desert.

"Look at the size of those trees!" I said. "They're huge. The pinecones are as large as my head. We've come to the land of giants."

"Are you going to do any gambling now that we're in Lake Tahoe?" John asked.

"No, I'll wait until we hit Las Vegas on the return trip."

This was the first tourist trap we stopped at, but having grown up watching *Bonanza*, I could not resist. It was what's known as a Potemkin village, constructed almost entirely of façades, with the saloon and family home being the only complete buildings. This was a good introduction to the Golden

State, where façades, smoke, and mirrors are a way of life.

San Francisco was the only place I mingled with people who were not tourists or catering to tourists. The hotel we stayed at provided accommodations for permanent as well as transient guests like us. While there, I became acquainted with some of the permanent guests. I met a Colonel Sanders lookalike and a man who dressed and talked like a pimp right out of the television show *The Streets of San Francisco*. While washing some clothes, I smoked a joint with some people in the laundry room.

"Ready for a drive?" John asked.

"I sure am. On TV, I watched police chases careening over the hills of San Francisco, but I never thought I would be there."

We crossed the Golden Gate Bridge on our way to the Muir Woods National Monument. The old growth redwoods are glorious. Some of those trees were old before Columbus came. Thank God some people decided to preserve a few of these giants of the forest for future generations to appreciate. Spending time among these guardians of the forest was a calming, spiritually moving experience.

About sunset, when we re-crossed the Golden Gate Bridge, rays from the setting sun turned the metal framework to gold.

We couldn't leave San Francisco without paying a visit to Fisherman's Wharf.

"It looks like every edible sea creature is available," John said. "It sure smells fishy. What are you going to try?"

"I don't know. I never ate seafood before."

"Try some of the jumbo shrimp and spicy rice."

I did. "It tastes a little rubbery, but enjoyable," was my comment. "Maybe I'll try seafood again."

We didn't let grass grow under our tires as we made our way to Los Angeles. We took the more scenic coast road. It's a slow, winding road, but there are plenty of overlooks to stop and watch the ocean.

"Listen to the breakers crashing against the rocks," John said. "It's amazing how many thousands of miles the waves roll before breaking on the California cliffs."

"Be extra careful," I told him. "This road winds along the cliffs like a snake, with no guardrails, and dusk is descending. I don't want to end up on the rocks being pummeled by the waves."

Sunset was incredible. The sun looked like a fireball sinking into the sea. It made the ocean look like it was on fire. I understood then why people praise the California sunsets.

Fighting our way through a traffic jam, we arrived in Los Angeles, land of dreams. The sheer number of tangled roads, overpasses, and underpasses awed me.

At Universal Studios, where fantasy abounds, we saw a mechanical shark, fire that did not consume buildings, cowboys that did not die when shot, and backlot sets that were hollow shells.

The staff made accessing the different venues at Disneyland while using a wheelchair enjoyable. I found the animatronics amazing. However, after a day of shows and rides, I became indifferent toward the various amusements. Disneyland appeared to be a soulless place where they worshiped the ingenuity of animatronics at the expense of people.

Having visited the major tourist sites in the Dream Capital of the World, we headed east, as John's vacation was quickly ending. Our next stop was the glitzy, glamorous city of Las Vegas.

If you want to gamble, this is the place. I couldn't afford to lose much, so I stuck with the slot machines. The best parts of

Las Vegas are the 99-cent buffet and the differently themed casinos. Toga-wearing servers, volcanoes spitting flames, and nightly light shows are all free to watch. With no clocks, money on display everywhere, beautiful people serving, and fantastically designed casinos, I felt alienated. Everything was a fantasy, designed to extract money, and if you want to participate in the illusion, you have to shell out. I couldn't fully participate in the fantasy because I didn't have the money.

Leaving the American dream behind, we headed into the primitive, lonely desert. Actually, it was a welcome relief to leave the hurly burly of the city. Coming upon Lake Mead, I felt like a Bedouin riding into the cool of an oasis after days on the desert. Surrounded by hot, dry earth, this ribbon of water looks fragile. If the people don't protect this valuable resource, it may no longer exist someday.

The next stop on our nature tour was the Grand Canyon.

"John," I asked, "what do you see when you look at the canyon from the overlook?"

"Not much. Mist obscures the bottom half of the canyon. No need for you to come out to look. The scale model in the interpretive center gives you the best understanding of the canyon."

Leaving the canyon, I asked John, "Why do people insist on destroying the pristine beauty of majestic natural wonders like the Grand Canyon, Niagara Falls, and the redwood forests by planting tacky tourist traps there?"

"It's all about money."

The Petrified Forest National Park was our last stop before making a big push for home. It's located in northeastern Arizona, and strewn around the sand are the most beautiful rocks I have ever seen.

"John, can you help me push the wheelchair through all this

sand? I want to feel that petrified log. Look at the vivid hues of purple, blue, yellow, black, and red running through the rock like veins. How did the wood turn to stone and become so colorful?"

"In the past, trees washed down from the nearby mountains," John explained. "Before they could rot, soil buried them. Chemicals in the ground turned the organic matter to rock, giving it the striking colors."

"It never fails to amaze me how Mother Nature created so much magnificent beauty for us to appreciate," I said, "but we're never satisfied. We try to improve on nature but usually fail. Thank you so much for inviting me on this trip, John. I had a fantastic time. I will never forget the beauty and majesty of the natural wonders I discovered on our journey. The sights, sounds, and smells I experienced on this trip will stay with me forever."

12
Romance and Fire

Once again, September found me back at university for my third year. Having pulled up my marks put me in a position to graduate that year with a BA. If I attained a high enough grade point average, I would enter the honors program the following year.

This would be my first full year in Village 2 after last year's precedent-setting move from Village 1. Since Village 2 accommodated mostly first-year students, I was at least four years older than the freshmen. All my friends from last year were now living off campus. If someone had told me that the next six weeks would be life altering, I would have laughed.

Staynor and Juggy, two of my best friends from the previous year, unwittingly rented a room from a slumlord. The property owner smashed a hole in the basement wall, joining two houses together, making fourteen bedrooms, five kitchens, and five bathrooms. With six women upstairs and ten men in the remaining rooms, there was no difficulty finding someone prepared to party any time of the day or night.

"John, do you want to come to the house for the weekend?"

one of my friends asked. "I told everyone about you. Keith, Barrie, Tim, the guys at the back, and the six women living upstairs all want to meet you."

"It sounds great. Especially meeting the women. What about returning to residence?"

"You can stay overnight. If we can't find you an empty bed, you can roll in with me."

Friday found Greg and me wheeling across campus and over broken sidewalks until we reached the rundown, faded yellow house. Peeling paint, cracked windows, missing shingles, and broken boards made it clear that the house was badly neglected. Inside, the house was a rabbit warren of small, shoddily constructed rooms, tiny bathrooms with leaky fixtures, and stoves with only one burner working. The place was a dump, but the social life was great. Students seem to thrive when making do.

Sitting around the kitchen table, Greg introduced me to some of the denizens of the party house.

"John, I want you to meet Theresa, Linda, and Debbie. They live upstairs with Katherine, Shirley, and Sandra."

"Hello, ladies. I'm pleased to meet you."

"Good to meet you," the women chorused.

"Call me Dee Dee," Theresa said. "All my friends do. When we were young, my brother could only say Dee Dee, so the name stuck."

"Where are you from?"

"I lived in Greensboro, Kentucky, until our family moved to Arnprior, north of Ottawa."

"What faculty are you in?"

"I'm in math. I like working with numbers."

"Great! You can come over sometime and help me with logic."

"I didn't think philosophy dealt with math. I thought all you arts people shunned us, but I'd be happy to help you."

"Accompany Greg on one of his visits," I told her. "That way you won't get lost. I can't guarantee how good my directions are."

The next Friday evening, Greg came for a visit, bringing Keith and Dee Dee.

"I told Keith about the Century Club," Greg said, "and he wants to join. Dee Dee and I came along to lend him some moral support."

"Did Greg explain the rules?" I asked. "A person keeps time, calling, 'Drink!' every minute. You then drink an ounce of beer. If you can't drink the ounce in that minute, you're disqualified."

"Sounds easy."

I laughed. "The first 30 or 40 minutes are, but then the going gets tough. Not wanting to see you drink alone, I'll join you."

"Can I be the timer?" Dee Dee asked. "I'll make sure you drink the ounce every minute. Greg had better pour the shots. After 40 or 50 ounces, you'll no longer be able to see to pour."

Greg poured, making sure there was a shot waiting when Dee Dee called, "Drink."

"This is going to be easy," Keith said. "I'm just getting started. Bring on the next shot."

"You just finished number 40; only 60 more to go."

"The beer isn't sliding down like the first 36 shots did. I feel dizzy. I think I'll throw up if I drink any more."

"Time! Forty-one."

Every minute Dee Dee called out, another ounce of beer went down Keith's throat.

Time! Fifty-nine.

Time! Sixty.

Keith couldn't finish the sixtieth shot. It and the contents of his stomach ended up in the plastic garbage can. Wanting to clean up and sleep, Keith headed home with Greg's assistance. The ordeal ended.

Upon their departure, I hopped in the wheelchair, heading for the bathroom. "I need water. My head is pounding, and my mouth feels like the Sahara Desert. Can I bring some back for you?"

"Yes, please."

Taking the water, Dee Dee patted the bed saying, "Sit down beside me. It's time for the logic lessons I promised earlier."

"The single bed doesn't give us much room to stretch out."

"Turn on your side. This is cozy."

Before I knew what was happening, we found ourselves wrapped in a passionate embrace. Questing tongues found mouths to explore. It didn't take long to wriggle out of our clothes, giving us access to each other's intimate parts. With tongues, teeth, and fingers, we explored each other's body. Breasts and belly, and I continued my exploration downward.

Consumed as I was by lust, instinct took over. Passion peaked. Tension broke, allowing our release.

With fulfillment came the most intense feelings of pleasure, desire, and love I could ever imagine. I was on Cloud Nine. I was in love.

With my having been a virgin, these were emotions I had never dealt with before. Had I found romance? Was this the beginning of a more permanent relationship? I hoped so.

"I really enjoyed our time together," I said. "It was special. You know what they say: You never forget your first lover."

"I'm not ready for a permanent relationship," Dee Dee said.

"I just found out that the jerk I dated in high school cheated on me for a year. I'm not ready to trust another long-term relationship as of yet. If I were, you would be the kind of person I would want. We can always stay friends."

In fact, we remained friends for years. I visited Dee Dee on her work terms. (She was in a program at the University of Waterloo in which schooling and work alternated on a semester system.) She visited me at my parents' home. People thought we were lovers, but we were close friends, which might have been better in the end. There was no bitter breakup. We remained friends until geographical separation caused us to lose touch.

With Oktoberfest in the air, one evening, Bud and Ricky dropped in for a visit with a 12-pack of beer. We rolled a few joints, chatting for a couple of hours.

Leaving a partial pack of cigarettes upon his departure, Ricky said, "Here, smoke a real cigarette. Forget those rollies. You won't have to spit out tobacco. Enjoy."

On my return from class the next afternoon, I stopped at my room on the way to supper. Seeing the mess from the evening before, I decided to clean up before going to eat. While hanging up my coat and collecting the beer bottles, I had one of Ricky's cigarettes. Before leaving for chow, I crushed out my cigarette, emptying the overflowing ashtray into the plastic trash container.

Returning from supper, I unlocked the door and rolled into the room. I was greeted by flames leaping from the plastic trash can. I realized that the ashtray I had dumped had started the fire. There was nothing I could do.

"My God!" I thought. "Look how fast the fire moves. It's engulfed the desk and bed. Get the hell out and pull the fire alarm!"

On the way out, I left the door ajar. This was the worst

thing I could have done. It allowed oxygen to enter the room, feeding the fire. Smoke also escaped, blackening the walls.

Outside, I was surrounded by the other residents, but I remained separate. Their excited chatter didn't penetrate my wall of guilt, fear, and sadness. Their joking banter only increased my isolation. For them, this was merely another adventure to tell friends about. For me, this would turn out to be life changing.

The babble in my brain wouldn't stop. "Will I have to pay damages? Will they charge me with arson? Will the residence administration throw me out? It's a horrible mess."

I felt humiliated. Everyone was staring, judging and blaming me. I didn't think I would remain in residence for another year.

Shortly after the arrival of the fire trucks, the fire marshal sought me out for an interview. Finding a quiet lounge, what I thought of as an interrogation commenced.

"Mr. Cronin, do you mind if I call you John?"

"No."

"I'm not here to assign blame. My purpose is to ascertain the cause of the fire. I only want to know if it was accidental or arson."

I understood that he wanted to put me at ease, but for what purpose? Did he want me to slip, thereby incriminate myself? I wasn't going to volunteer information.

"John, was your room where the fire started?"

"Yes."

"Did anyone threaten you or have a grudge against you?"

"No."

"Do you know how the fire started?" Seeing my hesitation, he continued. "Once more, I'm not looking to place blame. I only want to understand how the fire started and how it progressed."

Knowing I could hide nothing, I made up my mind to cooperate fully.

"Shortly before going for supper," I told him, "I crushed out the butt of a cigarette, dumping the ashtray into the trashcan. When I returned from supper, I saw flames leaping from the trashcan. I panicked, leaving the door ajar when I rushed out. If I had crushed out a hand-rolled cigarette, it wouldn't have continued to smolder the way the manufactured one did. I am so sorry. I don't know what's going to happen to me."

"Calm down, John. Here's a tissue. Things will work out. Do you have insurance? If so, it will help. I don't think I need any more information from you for my report. I hope things work out for you."

At last it was time to return to the scene of the accident. Stoically, I wheeled into the smoke-blackened room. My wheels crunched as I drove over the charred remnants of what had been my residence. The stifling scent of smoke and charred wood hung like a miasma over the room.

All the synthetic material and plastic furnishings had melted, leaving my stereo and mini fridge one amorphous mass. However, the wooden furniture made from two-inch pine was only charred. The heat from the plastics and synthetics was intense but short-lived. That's why the wood was only charred. However, the intense heat had caused cracks to appear in the cement block walls.

Continuing to survey the remnants of my soot-blackened room, my eyes came to rest on the soggy mass of ash covering the floor. There, amongst all the destruction, was an album cover, scorched around the edges, titled *Last of the Red Hot Burritos*. Later, I found out that while I wept for my loss, others were looting whatever they could. The next time I was in the campus center record store, I saw the results of their salvage operation. Hanging on the wall were four of my singed album covers.

That night, Tom, a good friend living on the second floor, offered me a bed. On the weekend, when Frank and I went home, I broke the news. I took a lot of flak for my careless smoking. They were right, but I was in no mood to hear what I already felt guilty for. Collecting some clothing, I returned to residence.

Staying in Tom's room was extremely inconvenient, given that he lived on the second floor. Within the week, Administration found a first-floor room that I could share. I remained in my new lodgings until the end of classes in April.

A few weeks later, I returned home for a family fund-raising party. The money raised help me get some new clothing, especially for winter. There were very few smoking comments made on this trip. With the passage of time, they ceased completely.

Knocking on my ethics professor's door, I heard "Come in. How can I help you?"

"I'm sorry," I said, "but my ethics paper will be late. Last month I had a fire in my room in residence. Ever since then, I've scrambled trying to get things together."

"I read about the fire in *The Record*, John. I wondered who the unfortunate person was. Now I know. There's no rush with the paper. Get it to me when you can. Good luck."

I did have good luck. My marks were high enough to get me into the honors BA program. I would be back for another year, but this time I would be off campus.

13
Blindness

My life underwent a major change when I entered the honors BA program. That is, I purchased a townhouse with my mother's help. Hoping to earn an MA and PhD, I faced six more years of school, so buying a house made sense. I planned to pay the mortgage by renting rooms to students. After three years of socializing at university, I thought I knew enough people to easily keep the rooms full.

Now that I was off campus, my commute to class was much farther than when I was in residence. Three times a week, I wheeled the mile and a half, up and down hills, to attend class.

When the weather was fair, my journeys were enjoyable. Fresh air, singing birds, and exercise made for a pleasant trip. In addition, there was the chance of meeting an interesting companion. What more could I want? When inclement weather struck, I opted for rides in the wheelchair transit van.

One winter day, while Greg pushed me to campus, a reporter for *The Record* took our picture for the next day's edition. I didn't know our picture was in the paper until Mom informed me of that.

Although I was free to wheel to campus and across the street to the plaza, I was no longer free to do so at night. My difficulty seeing in the dark progressed to the point where I could no longer recognize people at night. They were merely shapes.

The honors year passed quickly. With steady work, I achieved high enough marks to graduate in August 1979. I did not attend the graduation ceremony, preferring to wait until I graduated with a PhD. Thus, September found me enrolled in a master's program.

The department gave me a teaching assistantship. The pay was not grand, but it helped keep the wolf from the door. However, what I did gain was experience. For four terms of the next two years, I marked essays and exams, sat in on the class I assisted with, and helped students with problems. I hoped this experience would help me if I chose to teach.

Teaching and helping students with the material were easy tasks, but marking papers and exams was becoming difficult. I found myself struggling more and more to decipher some of the students' hen scratching. My own work suffered from similar problems. Making out the words when reading became more challenging. This meant that I took longer to complete assignments, and my comprehension was hampered. When writing essays, I no longer used a pencil, as the marks it made were becoming too faint for me to easily see. I used black ink and ensured that the characters were large and well formed. Although the work was becoming more difficult, I had to complete it if I wanted to earn the master's degree.

Why did I deny that I was going blind when it was obvious to any impartial observer that I was rapidly losing my sight? Why? Because I was not an impartial observer. If I accepted that I would soon be blind, everything I dreamed of would crash and burn. There would be no more hope, and hope is a marvelous motivator. If I buried my head in the sand, I thought, the problem would disappear, at least until sometime in the distant future. I would deal with it then and live today.

In the darkest part of the night, half awake and half asleep, like a nightmare, the consequences of my blindness reared their ugly head. Sleep ended and the night sweats commenced. On those nights, daylight was a welcome relief.

In the summer of 1981, I graduated with a master's degree.

"Mom, why do you want to go to the graduation and have a formal picture taken? In three years, I'll earn a PhD. I could wait and go to the graduation and have my picture taken then."

"John, how do you know you'll graduate again? You told me how difficult the work is becoming. Anne and Aunt Regina want to share in celebrating your achievement. We're all so proud of how far you've come despite all your problems. It would be selfish of you to deny Anne and Aunt Regina. I'll even take everyone out to lunch after the ceremony."

"You're right," I said. "Who knows what the future holds? Sharing the graduation with you, Anne, and Aunt Regina will make everything special."

To this day, I'm glad I listened to Mom. If not, there would be no memories to cherish and no pictures to commemorate the milestone. Young men don't like to admit that their mothers know best, but old men know the truth.

Immediately after graduation, I started the PhD program. I didn't want to waste time, as I had very little time to waste.

It was around this time that Mom and I sold the townhouse. With all my university friends gone, tenants were harder and harder to find. After the sale of the townhouse, I moved to an old, dilapidated farmhouse in the country. I shared the house with Webe, a friend from high school. He owned a car, which solved the ride problem.

The move to the concrete farmhouse was more of a withdrawal from society than a simple move. As a revolt against society, I started growing a beard. I also found myself neglecting my appearance. Trying to make my problems disappear, I started drinking and smoking more, but the difficulties always returned in the morning. I no longer cared what society thought. I felt that society had somehow failed me. I was angry and depressed.

Although my emotional state was in upheaval, I continued to do most of my course work. I completed the essays, but occasionally reading assignments remained unfinished. It was becoming more and more difficult for me to read.

In the summer of 1982, professors and teaching assistants gathered to mark logic exams. As I marked the papers before me, my thoughts turned bleak.

"Shit! Trying to see the answers to these True/False questions is difficult. I can tell whether the T or F is marked, but the next questions are impossible for me to make out. There are too many lines of faint scratches. Some students even used pencil. I can't see to correct the exam. I can't do my job. John, accept the fact that you're legally blind! No ifs, ands, or buts. You are blind."

With the realization came tears. Not many at first, just enough to dampen the exam paper. Before the dam broke, I wheeled to the nearest washroom and locked myself in a stall. Immediately the tears flowed like rainwater. Soon my frame was shaking with my sobs. Not long after, hiccups caused me to hyperventilate. Holding nothing back, I wailed out my pain, grief, and anger. I was desolate.

Slowly, ever so slowly, I began to regain control. Wheeling to the sink, I washed my face. I was thankful that no one had entered the washroom, as I didn't want my grief on display. Sympathy was not what I wanted right then.

After my departure from university, I never returned until I accompanied my nephew, 21 years later. University symbolized too many lost dreams and failures.

For days, I did nothing but mope around the house, brooding over my loss. What was I going to do? No school, no work, no money. I would be dependent on others for everything. Any way I looked at it, my prospects were grim. It was then that I remembered a conversation Webe and I had had.

"John, why don't you do a run to Jamaica? You could get a few pounds of hash oil strapped to your thighs and brace. With all the steel around you, they won't feel it when they search you. Get someone to accompany you on a cheap weeklong Jamaican vacation. I'd meet you down there and have the oil arranged."

At the time, I had replied, "Not me, Webe. I'm going to law school, or I'll teach university. I don't want to take a chance on getting a criminal record. I want a career."

But now, with all my prospects for a career dashed, I reexamined Webe's proposition.

"Should I do it?" I wondered. "Importing is a big step from selling small quantities to friends. But I wouldn't be doing anything I didn't previously do except getting the oil at wholesale prices. Making more money would ensure my independence."

I would also be carrying on a local tradition. During Prohibition and Depression years, the nearby Greenock Swamp had hosted bootleggers. I had heard the locals tell tales of how tasty their moonshine was. Although what they did was illegal, no one turned them in, and many enjoyed their product. I saw no difference between bootlegging and importing. The only difference was the product.

"Society wants to put me in jail for what I'm thinking of doing," I thought, "but it's legal to sell cigarettes and alcohol, even if many think their use is immoral. Therefore, just because some think the use of marijuana is immoral, that doesn't mean it should be illegal. The corollary, that because something is illegal it's immoral, is also false. For me, I can live with my conscience and submit to the law."

Wanting to make a new start, I abandoned the farmhouse, moving to Campbellville. It was there that I hoped to come up with a plan for the future. Whatever the plan, I didn't anticipate any forthcoming joy.

14
Importing

Having settled in at Campbellville, I started planning. Since I was blind, I hoped to get some help from the Canadian National Institute for the Blind. Shortly after I contacted the CNIB, a representative arrived with her driver. She gave me a stylus and hinged metal plates for brailling, paper to practice with, a braille alphabet, a talking book player, and a catalogue of book titles. They told me that a white cane and a guide dog were unavailable for me because I used a wheelchair. The talking book player and the tapes were a godsend, but the CNIB offered very little else. My prospects for a full, rich future were rapidly dwindling

Mulling the situation over, I finally decided to accept Webe's offer. I would meet him in Jamaica, where he would arrange for me to obtain marijuana oil to bring home. With my being blind and in a wheelchair, it would look suspicious if I went by myself. After pondering the problem, I thought of the perfect person to accompany me. Bud, a friend for years, had mentioned that he would like to go to Jamaica. It depended on whether he could escape from work. I decided I might as well phone and find out.

"Hello, Bud. It's John. How would you like to go to Jamaica for a vacation? It's not strictly a vacation, but more of a business trip. We would fly to Jamaica and return with some hash oil. I can arrange tickets and a hotel room if you're interested. All you need pay to pay for is the flight from Edmonton to Toronto and food. I'll arrange for the oil and pay you a quarter pound."

"It sounds like the same deal we spoke about when I last saw you," Bud said. "I'm in. When do you want me in Toronto?"

"Next Thursday. We'll fly to Jamaica on Friday. I'll arrange to have you picked up at the Toronto airport."

At dawn, a week after the call, Webe, Bud, and I dragged ourselves out of bed and headed to the Toronto airport. Checking in, security and boarding all went smoothly, and we were off to Jamaica.

When the cabin door opened, a wall of sticky, humid heat accompanied by jet fumes assaulted me. Immediately, I knew I was in a tropical land.

On our way to the Negril Beach Club for our week of fun in the sun, Bud asked the tour guide, "Can we drink on the transit bus?"

"No problem" was her response.

We quickly learned that "No problem" and "Soon come" were the two standard answers when replying to a request.

On our ride to Negril, when I looked out the window, I saw the ocean as a large blue patch, but I couldn't differentiate between sea and sky. People appeared as dark shapes, with no definition. The vegetation looked like an amorphous mass of jumbled green foliage. My eyes might be dim, but my nose was sharp enough to pick up the wood smoke from cooking fires. It reminded me of chimney smoke in the winter in Canada.

The next day, when Bud and I wheeled to the market, I

tried to make out the features of the Jamaicans hailing us. No luck. They appeared as dark shapes behind layers of filmy curtains. If they hadn't called out, I wouldn't have noticed them. Suddenly, it dawned on me. This was perhaps the last time that I would be able to make out faint shapes. This was my future. From that point on, I would have to depend on smell, sound, taste, and touch to make my way in the world.

Bud was a great companion. He didn't let me mope around the hotel room. He dragged me out, insisting we take advantage of what was available.

"John, I talked with a fisherman down the shore. He said he would take us out to the reef to snorkel for half of what the tour operators ask."

"I don't know. I'm afraid. I can swim, but I can't see where I'm swimming."

"No problem. The fisherman has a lifejacket. We can attach you to the boat so you won't drift away, and I'll be nearby."

"Okay. Let's go."

At the boat, Bud said, "You don't have to get out of the wheelchair. This strong man and I can lift you and the wheelchair into his boat."

Later, he said, "Here, let me help you with the lifejacket. I'll attach this rope to you and the boat. You're ready to go."

Grabbing me under the arms, Bud hoisted me over the gunwale, plopping me in the water.

Hitting the water, I made a big splash, yelling out, "This is fantastic. It feels warmer than my bath water. The water isn't deep. I can feel my feet dragging on the bottom."

Grabbing my tether, Bud pulled me closer to the coral reef. "Can you see anything, John?"

"I can see that something's there, but I can't make out color or detail."

As a substitute for my eyes, I constantly asked Bud to describe what he saw. I was especially interested in what he saw on the beach and by the outdoor shower. When he described the swimwear, I could hardly believe how tiny some of the suits were. A one-eyed pirate's patch was larger. It seemed that as my sight decreased, so did the size of the swimsuits.

As our vacation drew to a conclusion, Webe arrived at our hotel with his driver, Dudley. Previously, he had promised to take us into the country to see the real Jamaica. Picking up some parrot and doctor fish in Green Island, Dudley drove to his home district. Wanting to take us to an especially spectacular overlook, Dudley forced the ancient taxi to crawl up a steep, narrow dirt road. From the labored chugging of the engine, I was uncertain whether the vehicle would make it to the top of the hill.

"John," said Bud, "Dudley wasn't exaggerating! The view is spectacular! The hills descend in steps. I can't believe how far I can see. There's a boat maybe 20 miles from shore. Thanks, Dudley. The view was worth the trip."

Coasting down the hill, saving the engine, our next stop was a shop.

"This is like no bar I've ever been in in Canada," Bud said.

"What's it like?" I asked.

"It's a wooden shack with a metal roof. Can't be more than 150 square feet, with a plank bar at one end. There's no electricity, only a cooler with beer and ice. It looks like they also sell alcohol, along with soft drinks, and tinned or dry food."

"How are they going to cook the fish?"

"Dudley told me that an old woman is lighting a wood fire out back in order to make fish tea for us. I just hope she doesn't drink too much over-proof rum and fall into the pot."

"What's this fish tea?"

"I think it's what we call fish soup."

Waiting for our fish tea, Bud and I relaxed under a shade tree, drinking cold beer and smoking ganja. As I inhaled deeply, the scent of the nearby wild herbs reminded me of my mother's kitchen. I recognized sage, thyme, rosemary, and savory. But the fragrance of the herbs didn't mask the scent of shit from the horse parked nearby.

In the latter part of the afternoon, a commotion on the road brought me out of a half doze.

"What's happening, Bud?"

"It looks like the arrival of a bus full of schoolchildren. All their chatter sounds like the chirping of a flock of parrots."

"What do the uniforms look like? Each school has a different color scheme."

"The boys have yellow shirts with wine-red epaulettes and wine-red pants and polished black shoes. The girls have yellow blouses, wine-red ties and jumpers, and shiny black shoes. They look like a bouquet of flowers."

About an hour later, there was another commotion on the road. This time, they didn't sound like children. They sounded like a group of men on a mission.

Looking at Bud, one of the cane workers growled, "Ay, bwoy, why ya drinkin' in our bar? Ya belong in Negril."

Coming to our rescue, Dudley explained, "Oy, Winston, them be me friends. I bring them ta see my area and give Delroy's bar some business."

"If dem with ya, Dudley, dem cool. Don't drink all de beer."

With everything cool, it was time to taste the tea. Anticipating a delicious new Jamaican dish, I took a hearty swallow. Immediately, I spit out the vile concoction. It was a mass of mushy fish, bones, and vegetables. Throwing it out, I knew I could get a fine meal when I returned to the Beach Club.

Finally, the day of our flight arrived. The vacation was over, and it was time to pack the oil. Webe arrived at our room with the hash oil and weed.

"Webe, what the hell happened?" I demanded. "There should be a pound of oil for Bud to eat and two pounds for me to pack. All you brought is a half-pound of oil and an ounce of weed."

"That's all Shorty and Leroy made. They had some problems."

"I don't care. This trip is a total loss. Well, I guess it's too late to do anything about it except suck it up. But if do this again, you'd better come up with more reliable help. Bud and I are taking a risk for nothing."

"Too bad, too sad. I can't do better."

The time for complaining was over. It was time to get to work. Taking the triple plastic-wrapped, compressed marijuana, I slipped it down my briefs, tightening the brace's bellyband to keep the weed from slipping free. While I readied myself, Bud swallowed the 16 oil-filled condoms. Dressed, oil eaten, and bags packed, we were off in Dudley's rickety taxi.

Everything went as smooth as silk. There were no problems with immigration or security while departing. Arrival in Canada went off without a hitch. A friend picked us up, returning us to Campbellville.

"No problem," as they say in Jamaica, except for the screw-up with Shorty and Leroy. If I did this again, I would not use Webe and his bungling buddies.

With all the excitement over, I had time to reflect on my Jamaican experience. I found their lifestyle much more laid back than I was accustomed to in Canada. They made do with far less and were happy. Jamaicans appeared to be more accepting of my disabilities than Canadians were.

Could these differences in lifestyle provide the ingredients needed to help me accept my blindness? Could Jamaica hold the secret to the peace of mind I was searching for? The only way to gain a greater understanding of Jamaican life and culture would be to live in Jamaica for an extended period.

15
Living in Jamaica

For the next four years, I traveled, trying to outrun the consequences of the blindness. I was not only trying to outrun my difficulties; I was searching for something to give me peace of mind. After staying a couple of months in one place, I became anxious, needing to move, hoping to find that elusive something. I needed something to hold onto, to get me over this pain.

Traveling to western Canada, I stayed with my sister and various friends. Hoping to bury the problem, I tried to distract myself with drink, marijuana, and friends. No luck! There was no healing.

In my quest for peace of mind, I ran to Texas. Greg, a good friend from university, rented me a room. At times, I remained for two or three months. Again, I was hoping for that elusive something. Making new friends and drinking and smoking provided no consolation. Once more, I was disappointed.

Every winter, a friend and I returned to Jamaica. Each time, on my return, I brought oil home. After the screw-up on the first trip, I no longer engaged Webe to obtain and pack the oil. While living with Webe in the old farmhouse, I met Barrie. I found that

I could depend on him to deliver a quality product safely wrapped. The people I traveled with also agreed to use his services to obtain their oil.

I felt Jamaica had something to offer to help me accept my blindness, but I needed to stay for an extended period to find out. On every trip, I tried to reach this goal, but with no luck. I could stay at a guesthouse, but the cost of a long-term visit put that out of my reach. On each trip, hope rose but was soon dashed. To arrange an extended stay, I would have to form friendships with Jamaicans not residing in Negril.

In the winter of 1987, Bob, a close friend, accompanied me on my yearly trip to Jamaica. Being gregarious, Bob spoke with everyone he met. On one of his walks, he ended up at the Negril craft market, where he met Bunga Ray, a Rastafarian who ran a shop called Vital Ital. Every day around lunchtime, Bob returned to Bunga's shop for an Ital, a vegetarian meal of rice prepared in coconut milk with mixed vegetables. Soon, a friendship blossomed. When Bunga and others at the market gave Bob the nickname Ragamuffin, he knew he was accepted.

`"Oy, Muffin. Any time ya come back to Jamaica, ya can stay at me yard."

A few months after we returned to Canada, Bob took Bunga Ray up on his offer. Staying at Bunga's yard, it did not take the outgoing Bob long before he knew all the neighbors. One of the neighbors he met was Baby Lou. She lived atop a treacherously steep hill overlooking Bunga's house.

"Baby Lou, I have a friend in Canada named John. He wants to stay in Jamaica for a few months whenever he comes. However, he needs someone to help him. He's blind and can't walk."

"Him could stay here. Me can cook and clean fa him."

"One more problem. He can't get outside to the outhouse.

He has to bring a camp commode to use. Someone has to clean it out for him."

"No problem. Me can do everything fa him. Tell him ta come, and Baby Lou will take good care of him."

The first words out of Bob's mouth when I next saw him were, "I solved your problem. I found a place where you can stay for as long as you want. Bunga Ray said you could stay at his house. I also found someone to cook, wash, and take care of your needs. Her name is Madalynne Reid, but everyone calls her Baby Lou. She lives up a steep hill near Bunga's house."

"Thanks, Bob! Now I can find out what life in Jamaica is truly like. Are you positive everyone will be okay with the arrangement?"

"Yes. Baby Lou is looking forward to your visit. She wants to take care of you."

"Sounds great."

Encouraged by Bob, I decided to travel to Jamaica in September.

"How do I contact Bunga to tell him when I arrive?"

"You can't. He has no phone, and he doesn't return from Negril until early evening. Since there's no one around Bunga's house, you'll have to go to Baby Lou's and hope she's home."

As I passed through the Donald Sangster Airport, touts shilling for different taxis called to me.

"Oy, mun. Me take ya ta Negril. Ya can trust the I. Only one hundred to Negril."

As I sat in the wheelchair surrounded by bags, unable to see anyone, a nervous voice in my head warned, "Be careful. Because you're all alone, you're vulnerable. If the driver decided to rob you en route, there would be nothing you could do. You couldn't even identify them. But you need a ride to Lucea. You have to take a chance and hope for the best."

The Three Women Who Changed My Life

Turning to the voice, I called out, "I'm not going to Negril. How much to Lucea?"

"Oy mun, ya not a tourist? Tourists don't stop in Lucea."

"Back to the question. How much to Lucea? "

"Seventy-five U.S."

"I'll give you 80 Canadian. Take it or leave it."

"I'll take it. Climb in the van. What be ya name?"

"John. What do they call you?"

"They call I Junior."

During the ride to Lucea, my brain was abuzz. "I don't think the driver knows I'm blind. I can't believe my luck. A blind paraplegic going to the hills of Jamaica unattended. Now that I'm on the road, I only have to worry about arriving at Baby Lou's place. Will Baby Lou be home? What if she's not? I have no idea where to find her. If bad comes to worse, I'll have to continue on to Negril and hope to find Bunga at his shop. I'll have to wait there and get a taxi back to Lucea. What a screw-up that would be. Please, please be home!"

Having reached Lucea, I told Junior, "Take the first left after Freighter's Garage."

At the corner, Junior asked the shop owner, "Dis da road to Baby Lou's?"

"Ya, mun. Keep to the left when ya reach da Y. Her de second last house on de ill."

Turning around at the top of the hill, Junior parked at Baby Lou's gate, calling, "Oy, anyone about?"

"Ya, mun," came the reply from the veranda.

"Is dis Baby Lou's?"

"Ya, mun. I'm Baby Lou. Who be you?"

Yelling from the left side of the van, I replied, "I'm John, Bob's friend from Canada. He told you about me."

Shortly, Junior had the wheelchair, bags, and me deposited

on Baby Lou's veranda.

"Oy, driver, da ya want somethin' ta eat?"

"No, mum. I gotta get back to Mo Bay."

Grabbing the wheelchair handgrips, Baby Lou welcomed me, saying, "Come in now, mun. Me push ya. Da floor has some holes. Da ya wan some of me supper? Ya must be hungry after the plane ride."

"I sure am. What are you having?"

"Run down."

"What's that?"

"Fried salt pork, Irish potato, breadfruit, onion, and scallion."

"Sounds good. I'm starving."

While we ate, we got to know each other.

"Bob told me about ya. I know ya can't see or walk, but me don't care. I lost part of me hand in a bread-making machine."

"After Bob told me about you," I said, "I thought this would be my best chance to stay in Jamaica for a few months. He told me you could cook, and he didn't lie. This is great. The way Bob talked, you would also help me with washing and bathing."

"Ya, mun, I can help ya. No problem."

"Thank you, but there's something else I have to ask. It's not a pleasant request. I brought a portable camp commode because I can't get to the outhouse. I need someone to empty it and rinse it with bleach."

"I can do that for ya."

Before I realized it, dark had descended. As Baby Lou lit the lamp, I thought I heard a rustling outside.

Out of the night, a voice hailed the house. "Oy, anyone home? It's Bunga. Me come ta say howdy to Bob's friend, John. Oy, mun, glad ya made it."

"Thank you, Bunga. Everything is a little overwhelming."

"No problem. Here's a draw of ganja ta smoke. Tomorrow, Speedy will carry ya ta da house. Too dangerous in the dark."

"Thanks for the herb. Tomorrow."

Upon Bunga's departure, I rolled a cannon for Baby Lou and me to smoke. After finishing the spliff, it was time for Baby Lou and me to hit the hay.

Early the next morning, after a breakfast of açaí, salt fish, and plantain, I heard someone hailing us.

"Oy in there. Anyone up?"

"Ya, mun. We be up."

"Baby Lou, who's calling us?"

"Me brother, Speedy."

"Hello, all. Me here ta carry John down the hill ta Bunga's."

Squatting, allowing me to climb on his back, Speedy then carried me piggyback down the incredibly steep hill. Even with the steps cut into the hillside, Speedy needed to grab onto the bamboo to keep from sliding on the dry, loose clay. Reaching Bunga's house, Speedy lowered me, allowing me to flop onto the bed.

Returning later, Speedy told me that Peter Tosh's gardener had murdered him. I will always remember September 11, 1987 as my first day in Jamaica and the last day for a great Jamaican singer.

Alone and well rested, I was hit with the reality of my new lifestyle. No electricity, no running water, no telephone, and no toilet except my portable camp commode. I was living a primitive lifestyle compared to what I had left in Canada. What had I gotten myself into?

It didn't take long before I became part of the daily routine. Each morning, after breakfast, Bunga and his wife, Marva, were off to Lucea to catch the minibus to Negril. During the morning rush, Baby Lou brought my breakfast. While I ate, she emptied my camp commode.

"Dis be a two-cigarette job. The smoke helps take away de tink. Ya owe me a pack of Craven A."

"I can't thank you enough. Baby Lou. Without your help, I couldn't stay here. Here, this is enough for a couple of packs of Craven A."

With the chores completed, Baby Lou returned home, dressed, and went to Lucea to pick up what Marva had bought to cook for supper.

By mid-morning, I found myself completely alone. I found smoking ganja helped me pass the time. It made me content to sit and reflect on my life's choices and experiences. Listening to the talk shows and radio stories also helped pass the time. Another diversion was listening to books if the talking book player was charged. Every couple of days, Baby Lou took the large four-track cassette player to a shop for charging. It cost me about a dollar for a full charge.

After a few weeks of the same routine, I was in the groove. I knew they had accepted me when Speedy started calling me Johnny Cool. He gave me that name because I always answered "Cooling out" when anyone asked me "Whacha doing?" Everyone I knew in Jamaica had a nickname or alias. When addressing someone, I never knew if the name I used was correct or a pet name.

About this time, Marva started hinting that I should build a room beside the one I resided in. "Mista Cool, sometime American friends wanna stay wid us. If ya wanna stay long, ya could build another room beside dis one. Da room would always be here whenever ya come."

These not-so-subtle hints continued for a few weeks. Pondering the question, I thought, "If I continue coming fall and winter, having my own room would be useful. I would have a place to leave things to keep them safe. No more hotels. I might as well go ahead with the project. It'll save me money in the long run."

The job began when a burly young man arrived with his pick and shovel. In a couple of days, he leveled the site, dug out part of the hill, and departed. While Broad prepared the site, the local hardware store delivered cement blocks, bags of cement, marl, and gravel to the bottom of Bunga's hill. From here, workers carried all the material about 70 yards along a narrow path to the construction site. The last item brought to the site was water.

It didn't take long after the arrival of the mason and his helpers before they had the floor poured. This was the first time I had seen masons mix cement on the ground. Within the week, they completed the room.

As December approached, my time in Jamaica was rapidly dwindling. It appeared that all I would get from my new room was the scent of fresh concrete.

Finally, it was time to leave. The three pounds of honey oil I had ordered from Jimmy, a Rasta Bunga I knew, were ready. Taping some oil to the bellyband of my brace and wrapping some on each thigh, I strapped on my leg braces. I was ready to run the gauntlet.

At security in Montego Bay, I encountered no difficulties. After landing in Toronto, everything went smoothly. Soon I was at my parents' home, in time for Christmas.

Returning to Jamaica in January of the next year, since I arrived on a Sunday, my first stop was Bunga's place. When I reached my new room, I found everything the same as when I had departed. Immediately, I felt at home.

This comfortable feeling lasted until supper the next day, when Baby Lou made sure I understood her feelings.

"Me tired of up and down de ill. Every morning me go down de ill, bring breakfast, clean da commode, and climb up de ill. Then down de ill ta Lucea ta get what Marva leave for ya supper. Climb de ill, make supper, down de ill ta bring supper. Up da ill with dishes, and down de ill to stay with ya overnight.

"Me want ya ta give me de money ta buy ya food. Marva too mean. She keep da money left after buyin' ya food. She expect me to go up and down de ill and she keep da money. She be a wicked woman!"

"I don't know what to say," I told her. "I never knew that about Marva. It appears that she may be two-faced. I guess things will have to change. When I look at the situation, Marva does nothing for me except ask for money. Would moving up the hill to your house and giving you the grocery money solve the problem?"

"Ya, mun. No more up and down. Me have more energy for night work. Ya like me night work, so why not marry me?"

"I may have a difficult time getting you back to Canada."

"Not true! Ya ashamed of a one-handed woman."

"That's a lie. I'm disabled. Why would I shun you? It's the drinking. I went to Negril with Bob. When I returned, I found ya drank all the alcohol I kept the ginseng in. Ya have a drinking problem. I can't solve it. *You* must!"

The next day, after I told everyone about my move, Speedy once again hoisted me onto his back for the trek up the hill. With every step, I felt Speedy clutching the bamboo. By the time we reached the house, rivulets of sweat were pouring down his back. When he finally lowered me to the bed, it hit me. I had come full circle, returning to where I had started the previous year. This would be my new abode until I departed in early April.

16
Gilbert Crashes Ashore

Returning to the sundrenched island of Jamaica in September, once more I found myself at Baby Lou's house, perched high on the hill overlooking Lucea Harbour. While those below sweltered, balmy ocean breezes kept my eyrie cool.

On September 12, the raucous crowing of the nearby rooster rudely awakened me. Rolling over, I reached for the radio, turning it on just in time for the six o'clock news.

"The Miami Hurricane Center has issued a hurricane warning for Jamaica, Cuba, and the Caymans. Gilbert, the seventh named hurricane of the season, will make landfall in Jamaica about noon. The Jamaica Office of Disaster Preparedness and Emergency Management advises that everyone board up their windows, fill drums with water, collect nonperishable food, and move from low-lying areas and hillsides that are prone to mudslides. For those that must move, evacuation centers are located in most communities. Ask the local police for the location in your area. Remember, there will be high winds and heavy rain, so stay under cover for the duration of the storm."

"Oy! Baby Lou. Did ya hear the announcer? Sound like we're in for a big storm. Plenty of rain. We'll just stay put, smoke, eat, and have some fun together. The storm can't be that bad. By the way, what do I smell? Smells like plantain, dumplings, açaí, and salt fish. Let me at it. To hell with the storm. Sounds like Ragamuffin Bob made a good move by flying out yesterday. If he had stayed one more day, he would be stuck here."

By the time Baby Lou and I finished eating breakfast, Freddy and two of his friends arrived. As Freddy opened the door, it blew from his hand, slamming into the wall with a tremendous bang.

"Oy, Missa Cool! Da wind blow us away!" Freddy exclaimed as he and his two friends staggered into the house. "Da radio say Gilbert is on his way! Everyone ta board up window and get water and food," Freddy continued, fighting to catch his breath. "Baby Lou, what you need us ta do?"

"Notin', man," Baby Lou replied. "Me see storms before, and notin' bad happen. Just set some pans fe ketch da leak. Me goin' to cook now. Me wanna cook before the wind get bad. Da smoke from the coal pot will tink up the house. Ya wanna full belly wen da storm hit."

While Baby Lou prepared spaghetti sauce, Freddy's German friends practiced their English by quizzing me about Canada. Caught up in our conversation, I completely forgot about the storm raging outside. Every now and then, while talking about Canada and Germany, someone mentioned that the wind was getting louder and the sky was getting darker.

"Oy, Cool. Can ya hear da rain a–beatin' on the roof? It's a–gittin' worse. I hear tings a–bangin' on the ouse wall. De wind a–shakin' da ouse."

Cracking the wooden louvers open a smidgen, Freddy

gasped, "My Got! Da world a-gone mad. Da palm trees a-wavin' like old drunk walkin' home. Everyting a-flyin' around. Coconuts, dirt, leaves, even ya pan flyin' around like bird."

Although Freddy yelled while describing what he saw, I could barely hear him above the racket from the rain pounding on the zinc roof.

Yelling into my ear, Baby Lou shouted, "De spaghetti sauce be ready. Eat lots. Ya need strength for the storm."

Having filled my bowl with spaghetti, Baby Lou shouted to the others, "Come now, mun! Freddie, food be ready. Eat, mun!"

We ate our spaghetti dinner in silence, as conversation was impossible with all the noise. While I savored the food, I worried about what the storm had in store for us. With the last forkful of pasta, the house started to shake.

Suddenly there was a loud crack, immediately followed by the sound of rending wood and metal. Instantly, wind-whipped rain splattered into my face. Something terrible had happened, but I didn't know what.

Leaning over me, Freddy yelled in my ear, "Oy, Cool! I gotta move to da other side of da house! De wind lift de roof off one corner of da ouse! Everyting gittin' wet! We movin' everyting to da rooms on the side of da ouse overlookin' the hill."

Grabbing hold of the wheelchair, Freddy pushed me into one of the undamaged rooms. Now I was on my own, cut off from everyone by the uproar outside.

"This is one hell of a jam you got yourself into, John boy," I thought. "You're blind and can't hear a damn thing anyone says. You're at the mercy of the elements. You're completely dependent on others to keep you alive. You're scared shitless. Will you make it out of this hell alive? God only knows."

Suddenly the floor beneath my wheels began to shake! Hearing the loud crack of splintering wood, I knew the room had torn free from the house. As the floor tilted, the wheelchair and I started to roll. The wheelchair gathered speed. The walls had blown away, and I sailed out of the room.

"Oh my God, I'm gonna die!" I thought as the wind buoyed me aloft.

I was flying like a bird, but what about landing? Shit! I couldn't even see where I was going to land, but I damn well knew that jagged glass, splintered wood, and rusty nails were waiting for me.

As the flying wheelchair lost some of its momentum, it tipped forward, depositing me gently upon what had been the house wall. Thank God, none of the dangerous objects strewn around the hillside impaled me.

Although the wind and rain continued to pummel me, this was the first chance to gather my wits. It gave me a chance to calm down and assess my situation. My predicament looked grim.

Begging, I mumbled, "Our Father, Who art in Heaven, please spare me. Don't let me die on this cold, miserable hill."

I yelled, "Freddy! Baby Lou! Help me!"

However, my cries were useless. I was just pissing in the wind. The freight-train howl of the wind swallowed my frantic cries for help, but I continued yelling.

Soon, as I was hoarse from yelling and beginning to experience a mild case of hypothermia, there was more than rainwater running from my eyes. What could I do? I needed to get off that hill or die there.

Not liking my chances if I had to climb down myself, I screamed, "Baby Lou! Freddy! Help! Me need ya help!"

Straining my ears, I thought I heard a faint voice reply, "Oy, Cool, me soon come. Hang on."

Relief washed over me. Someone had heard. I didn't

recognize the voice, but help was on the way. Maybe I wouldn't die there after all.

Suddenly Baby Lou had me in a bear hug, blubbering into my ear. "Cool, ya alive! Me see ya fly out a da room. Me thought ya died." Squeezing me even harder, Baby Lou wept, "Thank God ya alive. Me not know what me do if ya get killed."

"Top the bawling, Lou!" Freddy demanded. "Are ya iray, Cool?"

"Me iray," I cried in reply. "What are we going to do?"

"We get down de ill to Bunga's house. We'll be safe der. Let Baby Lou and me carry you down the ill." Freddy and Baby Lou grabbed me under the arms, dragging me to the lip of the hill.

"This is not going to work!" I shouted. "You can't even stand up, let alone try to carry me! We'll each have to try to crawl down the hill on our own."

"This is going to be one hellish trip down," I thought. "Even during dry times, with the steps cut into the clay, a person has to cling to the bamboo for support. Can I avoid all the broken glass and punji like splintered bamboo littering the margins of the path? With torrents of water falling from the sky, turning the trail into a water slide, can I make it down safely? I have to dig my fingers deep into the saturated clay to keep from washing away in the current. Concentrate on each hand hold. Make sure you're secure before pulling your hand from the sucking ooze. Next handhold. Slow but sure wins the race and keeps me alive."

Reaching the bottom of the hill after what felt like an eternity, I finally grasped how much water was pouring down the hill. At the nexus of the downhill trail and the track to Bunga's, a mini-waterfall had formed. I found myself sloshing around in a raging, two-foot-deep torrent. The flood was too deep for me to fight through if I wanted to get to Bunga's house. With no hesitation, Baby Lou and Freddy grabbed me under the arms and half-carried, half dragged me through the deluge to the nearby house.

Seeing us coming, Bunga Ray's wife, Marva, flung open the door just as we arrived. Hustling us into the house, she brought us towels.

What a relief to be out of the slashing rain and gale force winds! To help me calm down, Bunga offered me a marijuana spliff, but I shook too badly to light it unassisted. Seeing me shake, Marva offered me a jacket. After we had caught our breath and dried off, we commenced blurting out our adventure. Before I got three words out, though, a furious gust of wind smashed against the house, causing the entire structure to shake.

Over the shrieking wind, Bunga Ray yelled out, "Blood clot, mun! De roof a fly off! Oy, mun! Tie et down! Marvie! Go inna de basement! If the roof lif off, me want everyone in de bottom rooms."

As Freddy and Bunga Ray struggled with the roof, I dragged myself to the trap door leading to the basement. Being the youngest, Mikey and Renée were the first through the trap door, down the ladder to the two lower rooms. Baby Lou was next. She would be able to catch me if I fell while going down the ladder.

Just as I started climbing down the ladder, an especially violent gust of wind crashed against the building, rocking it to the foundation. From the terrible screech of rending wood, I knew the roof was ripping away from the house. Immediately, wind assaulted me and rain lashed my face. Heedless of splinters, I slid down the ladder, whereupon Baby Lou grabbed me, dragging me to the bed, where I joined Mikey and Renée. The way the water poured through the trap door and the ceiling, it was obvious that the house no longer had a roof.

Above the roar of the storm, I heard Marva scrambling down the ladder, followed by Freddy and Bunga Ray. With the bang of the trap door locking, I hoped we would be safe.

Our new refuge consisted of my original room and the room I had built. The rooms had wooden louvered windows and doors to the outside, plus a door connecting the two rooms. The sparsely furnished rooms contained mattresses on wooden frames and some chairs. Ordinarily, a kerosene lamp or candle provided the lighting, but no one had had time to bring either. These small, Spartan, stygian quarters would be the home for Marva, Baby Lou, Bunga Ray, Freddy, Renée, Mikey, and me for the remainder of the storm.

Baby Lou, Freddy, and I took up residence on the bed in the room I had had built, while the others remained in the room with the trap door. Although the storm no longer battered us, we still got wet. There was a constant drizzle falling from the ceiling.

Nudging Baby Lou, I grumbled, "Me soaked. The bed soaked. There is no way ta escape the damn rain. If Freddy don't bail the water out, it'll be up to the mattress. It's not bad enough that we got blown out of the house. Now we gotta put up with being constantly wet. I can't take it."

"Try this," Baby Lou suggested, as she handed me a sheet of plastic. "It'll elp keep da watta off ya."

"Okay. I'll try anything to get away from de water."

In a short time, my muffled voice said, "Dis is not working. The plastic makes me hot, and it doesn't stop the water. The humidity forms on the inside, making me wet. I'm no further ahead. Here! Take it away. At least I'll be cooler."

The cement walls and the ground helped deaden the tremendous din from outside, allowing us to hear each other. We made a desultory attempt at chatting, but everyone was preoccupied with his or her thoughts. I soon fell into a light doze from the fatigue that followed my prolonged adrenalin rush.

Hovering between semi-wakefulness and dreams made for a fitful sleep. I couldn't shake the haunting fear caused by the trauma of the last few hours. Would the storm shatter our refuge for a third time? I wouldn't rest easy until the storm abated, and even then, it would be a while before fear of a hideous death no longer haunted my dreams.

Suddenly, a battering at the door yanked me from sleep.

"What the hell is happening now?" I wondered. "Is Gilbert battering down the door, trying to blow his way in? Do I have to get ready to fly again? No, I think I hear a voice. Who would be out in this storm? I hear Bunga sloshing through the water, so I'll soon know. It's Aunt Lou, Baby Lou's aunt! If she's here and not at home, that means her little house is gone. I bet she's got a tale to tell."

After settling into the chair, Aunt Lou commenced to tell her tale of terror.

"Me sittin' at me table wid the candle a-flickerin. I prayin' de Lard ta spare me life. A hard breeze come blow off de housetop! Da wall fall in a crop off the hole a me foot. Me gotta fight me way thru de watta on the path ta get 'ere. Me almost drown."

"That was one lucky woman," I thought. "With the walls and roof crashing down around her, she was lucky not to be seriously injured. All she suffered were a sprained ankle and some minor cuts and scrapes on her legs and arms. She lost her house, but not her life."

With the excitement generated by Aunt Lou's arrival fading, boredom and misery again consumed me. It didn't take long before I again slid into a light doze.

Once more, hammering on the door dragged me from

sleep. This time I may have been startled, but not frightened.

"Who is it now?" I wondered. "If someone is at the door, that means another poor soul lost his or her house."

Feeling the bed shake, I knew Freddy had gone to let another refugee in. Hearing the voice, I knew Mandoon had arrived. When he settled himself, I knew we were in for another sad tale of loss.

"Me sit dung at me table. Big breeze come a–blow off de ouse top. Me almost blow away when da roof lif off. De walls, dem stay up. Me almost wash away gittin' here."

Hearing the story, I thought, "Mandoon is a lot luckier than Aunt Lou. His walls didn't collapse, and he escaped without a scratch. We now have nine people in our cramped refuge. Who else will show up?"

With exhaustion and boredom returning, it didn't take me long to fall asleep. At some point, I slowly surfaced from my nightmarish dreams.

I asked myself, "Why did I wake up? There's no one banging at the door. What's wrong? I don't hear anything, so what's the problem? That's it! I can't hear anything. No howling wind! No rain battering the ceiling! Could the storm be over? Could we be that lucky?"

Aloud, I said, "Oy, Bunga! How long we been down here?"

"It's eleven o'clock," was his tired reply. "We be down here near eight hours."

"Do ya think the storm is over?" I asked.

Before Bunga could reply, someone knocked at the door.

As Freddy pulled the door open, a voice boomed out, "Oy! Everyone alive?"

"That must be Speedy, Baby Lou's brother," I thought. "Did their house blow away? What about Eiki and Farina? I hope no one was injured."

"Me come ta see if everyone iray."

"Everyone iray in here, but we be wet," Bunga replied. "How be Eiki and Farina? What about da house?"

"Eiki and Farina da safe, but the rass ouse try ta fly away. The wind lift the ouse up, but not tip over. All the time Farina a-bawlin' out. She afeared the ouse fly away with her. All the time Eiki a-tryin' to cool Farina down."

"Da ya have any news about da storm?" Freddy asked.

"Me hear on the radio dat the storm a-beaten Jamaica somethin' terrible. Right now, da eye a passin' over Jamaica. I gotta get back before da storm hit again. Must take care of Eiki and Farina. Don't wanna blow away. Everyone keep iray."

"Iray. Ya stay cool. Hail up Eiki and Farina for us," we called out as the door slammed shut.

Shortly after Speedy departed, the wind started screeching like a buzz saw. This time, the storm didn't slowly build to a crescendo. It burst like a bomb. It was only half over. We had another eight hours of mind-numbing boredom, entombed in the absolute darkness of the basement. With no distractions, tedium and exhaustion lulled me to sleep once more.

Hoping to make the time pass faster, I tried to sleep for the next eight hours. This was a dismal failure. With every disturbance, I came awake, anticipating some new disaster.

On one of these occasions, I lay for a moment, confused, wondering what had woken me.

I thought, "Silence. No howling wind. No drumming rain or crashing thunder. The storm is over."

"Thank God we made it through the storm unscathed!" I joyfully shouted.

Note

For more information on Hurricane Gilbert, go to
https://en.wikipedia.org/wiki/Hurricane_Gilbert

17
Aftermath

Neither the demonic shriek of Gilbert's winds nor the drumming of rain on zinc roofs assaulted me any longer. The ferocity of the hurricane evaporated, leaving us with mud, blue skies, and a furnace-like heat. We had endured the worst hurricane the Caribbean could throw at us.

Soon my companions threw open the windows and doors, allowing the bright sunlight in, dispelling the basement gloom. They quickly made their way to the wet, sunny outdoors, but I had to remain inside because I didn't have my wheelchair.

Needing to know the wheelchair's condition, I called out, "Oy, Freddy! Can you go up the ill and look about my wheelchair? I'm fretting something terrible. What if it's all smashed? Me can't rest until I know."

"Ya, Misa Cool," Freddy replied. "Me go back up the ill and see what me can find."

"Me comin' too," Baby Lou piped up. "Me wanna see what left of me ouse. Me can 'crape up whatever I can before the thiefs take everythin'."

Later, hearing voices, I cried out, "Baby Lou! Freddy! Are

you back? Did you find the wheelchair in one piece? Say something, mun. Me so nervous, me shaking."

With a huge smile in his voice, Freddy called back, "No problem, mun. We got da chair. It in one piece. Me drag it down the ill. Me clean off de mud afore ya use it."

"We got ya ticket and passport," Baby Lou continued. "Me find pillows, sheets, and blankets. Me gonna hang this stuff on da bushes ta dry. Won't take long in dis eat."

I could hardly wait to escape my prison. Immediately upon Freddy bringing the cleaned wheelchair to me, I leapt into it, asking him to push me out into the daylight. As I emerged from the dark cellar, the blistering hot sun assaulted me, while blue skies and gentle breezes greeted me. What a relief to be free from my basement cell! In no time, I was dry and warm. Any lingering fears I harboured concerning the storm blew away in the gentle breeze. With the heavy burden of fear lifted from my shoulders, I felt free. Now that I was warm and dry, it was time to take stock of my surroundings.

"Oy, Freddy. What da ya see? What did Gilbert smash? What is left standin'?"

"Misa Cool, every tree, bush, and line is strewn with clothing and bed stuff. Look like white bird flappin' in the win. Mattresses layin' in every yard. Most trees gone. No shade!"

"It's going to be hot for a long time with no shade," I said. "Are the roads blocked? Are we cut off from Mo Bay?"

"I don't know," Freddy replied. "With all the trees and wire down, current will be gone."

"No problem," I said. "We had no current before Gilbert. At least all the drum pans and the tank are full of water. We can drink and wash. That's the only good thing Gilbert did." I was trying to look on the bright side.

Once again, Freddy and Baby Lou trudged up the hill to

salvage what they could before the looters came. Upon their return, I received a full description of the salvage and the destruction.

"Blood clot, mun! The ol ouse is a pile of wood. Me tings spread all over the ill. Clothing here! Dishes there! Tank God the dishes not smashed, just thrown all over da place. Me got da mattress. Most of the ol' furniture broken. Me don't know what to do," Baby Lou wailed as tears ran down her cheeks. "Me got nothin'!"

Hugging her, I tried consoling her, saying, "I'm here for you. We can rebuild your house. Clothing and bedding will dry out. You didn't have much furniture, and what you did have was worn out."

Freddy joined in, saying, "Lou, thins will work out. Ya still got ya friends. People will elp ya."

After Baby Lou calmed down, Freddy continued his inventory of what they had found, saying, "We got ya braces, wheelchair cushion, and clothes. I found the book player and tapes, but dem well wet. Can try to dry it out."

In the mid-afternoon, Merrick returned from Lucea. The last time I had seen him, Merrick and Freddy's German friends were running from the house as it collapsed around us. With Merrick's arrival, we received news from the outside world.

"Oy, Merrick, where did you go when you ran from the ouse?"

"Me and the German boys run down the ill to the all age school. Me get there and squeeze me big botty into the pickney desk. Before I get set, the roof lift off. I spend de whole night squashed into a likkel seat, with the rain a-pourin' down on me. A rass bad night."

"Merrick, what ya got? I hear somethin' clinking."

"Scotch, bully beef, coffee, some rice, and corn meal.

Everyone down to the Hanover Agency gittin' what de can. I saw Bagga leavin' with a sack of flour. Everyone 'crapin' up whatever de can. Mostly food. With da roof off the Hanover Agency, not long before every ting rotten. All de little people gettin' food, but de cops loadin' up big stuff. Ya should see it. Dem police boys a fillin' up the police Jeeps with TVs, stereos, fridges, stoves, and fans. Dem police boys is thiefs."

"You're right on," I replied. "I know ya cannot trust dem police boys. What else happening in Lucea? What about the roads?"

"Everythin' tor up. Road to Mo Bay and Sav blocked with torn up coconut trees. No current in Lucea. Power lines ripped down. Water pipes still good, but no current to run pump."

"No problem. We had no current or running water before the storm, so we won't miss them," I said with a smile.

Our major source of news came from the radio. We learned it took three days to restore travel between Lucea and Montego Bay. Another interesting detail I learned from the radio was how the loss of so many trees would affect the ground. The loss of the tree cover would allow the land to become hotter, leading to less food production and a decrease in the number of coconuts.

The first big task was to get a roof on Bunga's house. Until we accomplished this, we were getting soaked every time it rained. This would not be easy because of the shortage of boards, corrugated metal for roofing, hardware, carpenters, and money.

"We need ya to elp with the roof," Marva stated in her no-nonsense manner. "Everythin' expensive. We need some more money."

"I'll see what I can do," was my curt reply.

Having overheard our conversation, Baby Lou wailed, "What about me ouse? Ya stay up to de ouse, and now it gone. If you give dem all the money, me ouse not get built. Where will ya stay then?"

"I understand where ya comin' from," I said. "Marva always dingin' me for money. I'd sooner work on your house, but we need a roof over our heads. I'm wet whenever it rains and damp whenever me not in the sun. We can work on your house when the roof is on Bunga's house. If ya wait, ya might get some of the things sent from foreign."

"Me not happy."

"I know, but me can't do better. We need a dry place to live until we can build your house, and I'm the only one with some money right now."

With some help from me, the roof went on in two weeks. Luck was with us, since not much rain fell while the roof was being completed.

During the roof repair, I lived in the wheelchair, eating and sleeping there. This and the dampness from the intermittent rains caused my skin to break down. One afternoon, while preparing for my shower, I asked Baby Lou to look at my sore bum.

Looking at my butt, Baby Lou shook her head, saying, "Not lookin' good, mun. Ya skin gettin' watta bumps. Ya gotta take care not ta get pus in dem sores. Me gonna pick some bush ta put in the watta ya bathe in. Me den set de pan of watta in the sun with da bush in it. It'll keep da skin from getting worse."

Lowering myself into the pan of warm water, I exclaimed, "Ooh, yes! That feels great. Thanks, Lou. I can feel the medication soothing me butt."

"When ya done, me dry ya off good. When the butt dry, me put on some baby powder. It'll keep ya dry."

After a few days of the treatment, my bottom began to heal. The pain decreased, and most of the water bumps disappeared.

Being able to lie on a clean, dry mattress hastened my recovery.

One afternoon, while I was soaking in the dishpan, a couple of people hailed me, saying, "Hello, Cool. How are you? What did you do with all the trees? It looks empty."

Immediately I replied, "Johnny P! Swinging Bob! What the hell are you doing here? Don't ya know we just had a hurricane? Ya must be crazy."

"We know. We didn't want you to have all the fun. What a difference a couple of weeks make. When I left, everything was lush, with a lot more trees."

Coming to where I soaked in the dishpan, Johnny P asked, "Are you all right? Did you get hurt in the storm? You look okay."

"I made it through Gilbert without a scratch. The problem came with the aftermath. Sitting in the wheelchair in the damp made my butt sore. That's why I'm soaking in this pan full of water and leaves. It's working. I'm getting better."

During the next week, I regaled Bob and John with my adventures. All too quickly, the week passed. It was time for them to head back to Canada, but they worried about leaving me.

"John, are you sure you won't come home with us? I feel guilty leaving you here. We can change your ticket," John coaxed.

"No. I gotta wait for the oil."

"You can pass on this one," Bob cajoled. "Make it up on the next trip."

"The oil is just my excuse for staying longer," I told them. "The truth is, I'd feel guilty leaving everyone I shared the disaster with. I would be running out on my friends. I understand how soldiers bond during war, hating to leave their buddies in the field. That's how I feel."

"Okay, you're the boss. One last chance," Bob and John

chorused. "Since you're not coming, we'll see you at Christmas."

With the roof on Bunga Ray's house and building supplies flowing into Jamaica, Baby Lou demanded, "When ya gonna start de ouse? Me no wanna stay in another's ouse. Me want me own."

"Well, go ta de PNP office and see if they'll give ya some vouchers," I retorted. "Ya got a brother in de party. Tell him ta help ya get vouchers so ya can rebuild. I heard he gotta pile of zinc roofing hidden under his house. Tell him to give ya some."

"I don't like a beggin' from dem people. Dem all ignorant and greedy. I don't support dem party, but I'll go and try."

Hearing Baby Lou as she returned from town, I called out, "How did ya do? How much money and vouchers did they give ya?"

"None! Dem rass clot boys tol me ta get the white man ta help ya! Dem give me nothin'. Dem not put me name down ta get somthin' later. Dem wicked!"

"Ya brother won't give ya anything?"

"Not one bumbal clot sheet of zinc. Him a greedy bastard!"

"This whole distribution is a scam," I told her. "Party hacks and dem friends get vouchers! Look at Cherry. She owned nothing and she got vouchers. I wonder what she gave dem. I hope it was a dose. So, no help fa ya. All these donations from foreign, and ya can't get a bloody thing. Corruption and payoffs! Well, I guess if anything a gonna get done, it's going to be up to me and your people in America and Canada. Get on the phone to Babs and Fitty in Toronto, Silk in St. Pete, and Sandra in Miami. This bumble clot government set up this system to make corruption easy!"

With money from family and me, Baby Lou purchased some of the material she needed to rebuild. She also hired Boppa, the same carpenter Marva had used to put on her roof. At various times during the day, Baby Lou checked on the house, ensuring the carpenter didn't steal anything. On one of these trips, even though I was at the bottom of the hill, I could hear Baby Lou cursing.

When Baby Lou returned, I asked, "What's all the cussin' about?"

"Dem tiefin' boys trying ta rob me. Dem a hidin' boards in da bush. In de evenin', dem take da boards ta Mandoon's ouse, hidin' dem under da ouse bottom. Me gonna fire dat worthless boy!"

"I wish we could. But if ya fire him, where will ya get another carpenter? All we can do is make sure Boppa and his aprento, Mandoon, can't get a chance to tief. Ya know their tricks, so keep a watch on dem."

Despite thieves, government corruption, and a shortage of money, Baby Lou had four walls and a roof over her head when it came time for me to depart for Canada.

"What do ya think, Baby Lou? It still needs paint, windows, and partitions inside, but the doors and the plywood covering the windows will keep out da weather until I get back. When I return, we can put windows and partitions in. I'll bring a solid lock for the door."

"It not big like the other ouse, but more solid. De ouse don't shake when ya walk on the floor. It's plenty hot with no windows."

"It's only for a short time, just until I get back. Stay with Blanche if it gets too hot."

"When ya get back, we could get married."

"We don't want to rush into anything, Baby Lou. I'll see when I return."

With the approach of Christmas, I prepared to return to Canada. This time, I welcomed my return, wanting to escape the sordid corruption. The entire episode had thoroughly sickened me. However, with all the wealth floating around, this would turn out to be the best Christmas Jamaicans had experienced in years.

18
Further Adventures in Jamaica

Over the next three years, I visited Jamaica every winter and fall, returning to Canada in the spring and at Christmas. On these trips, there always seemed to be some harrowing incidents, but none as horrendous as my battle with Hurricane Gilbert.

On a visit in the winter of 1989, it became obvious that Baby Lou's yard needed chopping. Bamboo and grass were taking over.

"Me need a thousand Jamaican ta pay Marva's man ta chop da yard and 'crape everything up."

"Here's the money. Make sure to tell the man to be careful. Everything is bone dry."

"Ya, mun. Me tell da man ta start, then go ta Lucea ta buy somethin' to cook fi ya supper. Freddy will stay wid ya while me gone."

While Freddy and I visited, the worker swung his machete and scraped up the trash.

"Hey, Freddy, what's the crackling sound? I think I smell

smoke."

Standing, Freddy looked between the window's louvers, exclaiming, "My Got! Da rubbish is burnin'. Me run ta Shirley's shop. She got a phone so me can phone the fire brigade."

While Freddy sprinted along the path to Shirley's shop, I climbed into the wheelchair, pushing myself onto the veranda.

"Oh, my God!" I thought. "It sounds like the snapping and popping sounds are getting closer. I wish I could see so I'd know how near the fire is. Not seeing how close the flames are makes everything worse. The smoke smell is increasing. I feel the air becoming hotter. The fire must be nearby. I hear the fire truck coming up the hill. The ooga, ooga of the truck's air horn is getting louder. Please hurry!"

As the truck stopped at our gate, I heard the firefighters' boots hit the ground as they leapt into action. One group hosed down the rubbish pile, while others dug and beat out embers. It was not long before they had the fire under control. Before leaving, they filled up our drums with water in case there were any flare-ups.

Although everything worked out for the best, I continued shaking like a leaf in a windstorm even after the firefighters had departed.

"Calm down, Misa Cool," Freddy said. "It be over. Ya safe."

"I know. But I can't get visions of smoke and heat out of my head. I still feel like the flames are licking around me, trying to roast me alive." Taking deep, calming breaths, I slowly regained control. "It will be a long time before I forget the horrors of this fire!"

On her return in the mid-afternoon, Baby Lou exclaimed, "Blood clot! What happened?"

"What happened? I'll tell you!" I said. "Your worker threw a cigarette into the trash pile. If you hadn't been downtown drinking all afternoon, you'd know what happened. If not for Freddy, I'd have burnt alive."

"Not me fault. It be the blood clot feebleminded worker. Me gotta go to town ta buy food fa supper!"

"No! That's just an excuse. Bob brought the big cooler, and Merrick brings up a block of ice twice a week. Ya could buy enough for a few days, but ya just wanna drink with ya cronies! Ya keep talking about marrying, but ya cannot stop the drinking."

"Me do better. No need ta go a town for the rest of the week. Me stay home and cook."

On a trip the next year, I fell prey to a sneak thief. While I was relaxing in my recliner wheelchair, Monica, a friend of Baby Lou's, stopped by for a visit. I told her Baby Lou was sleeping, but she still barged into the house. After a few minutes she departed, saying, "Me can't get Lou up. Too much rum."

I didn't give Monica's visit a second thought until the next morning. "Baby Lou, here's a hundred dollars to change. But something doesn't feel right." Recounting the money, I exclaimed, "I'm a hundred short. Who would take it? The only person who was here was Monica."

"No, she wouldn't teef da money. We ah friends fa years."

"Well, I think she did. She strode into the house as if she owned it and tried to wake you, but you were too drunk. When you go to Lucea, get the money back from her. None of this would have happened if you didn't get drunk all the time."

Reaching downtown Lucea, Baby Lou confirmed my suspicion. She saw Monica, who didn't have a pot to piss in, buying food and drink for herself and some friends. It was obvious she was the thief. Threatening Monica with arrest, Baby

Lou had her sign a paper in front of a Justice of the Peace admitting she stole the money and promising to repay it.

Putting the incident behind me, I accepted that I would never see the money again. However, this was not the end.

When Bunga heard what had happened, he told Bob, "Oy, Muffin, get da oil and herb out of da house. Monica be spiteful. She gonna send a police boy around."

Heeding the warning, Bob and Freddy moved all the weed and oil to Freddy's shack. That afternoon, while I was relaxing on the veranda in the recliner wheelchair, a taxi stopped at our gate, dropped a man off, and waited.

"Oy, ya on the veranda, don't move. Ay, boy. You in da kitchen, stay where ya are. Me lookin' fe drugs. Da only warrant I need is right here." He chuckled as he patted the holstered pistol.

"Ya won't find anythin' here," Baby Lou piped up. "But me keep me eye on ya while ya look. Me know how ya police boys work."

Finally, after 45 minutes of emptying, poking, and prodding baskets, boxes, and dressers, the man departed, finding nothing. "Ya lucky dis time, but me got me eye on ya."

I found out that the cop owned a taxi in Montego Bay that needed repairs. A quick shake down of a tourist, and the cab is on the road again. However, this time, he had no luck.

The next year, one fall evening found Baby Lou, Freddy, and me sitting on her veranda enjoying the cool, balmy Jamaican breezes.

"Do I hear a vehicle coming up the hill?" I asked.

"Me see lights," Freddy replied. "Yes, it's the police Jeep."

"What do they want now?" I asked. "Never good news when dem boys around. They make me nervous. Are they comin' to search the house again?"

"Don't worry, Cool," Baby Lou said. "Dem drive past the gate. Dem turn at Delroy's and comin' back. Now dem stoppin' at the cane patch. A couple of dem police boys gon inta the cane."

"Why? What's going on?" I quizzed.

"I don't know, but dem leavin' real fast," Freddy replied. "Somethin' frightened dem boys. They can't get away fast enough."

Why were the police in the cane patch? Before we could solve the riddle, the police Jeep returned. This time, four officers accompanied the Jeep. With each visit, there were more officers. There was something very interesting in that field of sugarcane.

Early, before cockcrow, someone began pounding on the side of the house.

Half asleep, Baby Lou hollered out, "Who dat wakin' me from me bed? Ya betta have a good reason fer wakin' me up!"

"Lou! It's me, Sweeny. Did ya hear about the hangman? Some pickney playin' in the cane patch across de road found a man hangin' in a tree. The pickney run to the station and tell the police. Did ya see da police comin' up here last night? Hurry up, Lou. Get up and come ta see the hangman. A whole bundle of people gonna be comin' up the hill ta see him. I gotta go. Wanna see the hangman before the crowd. Me gone."

With that, Sweeny departed like Paul Revere to spread his news of death.

Sleep was out of the question after Sweeny's visit. Before Baby Lou had time to open the door to the veranda, the police Jeep returned for the third time. With the police setting the tone for the day, the crowds soon followed.

While we ate our breakfast of açaí and salt fish, what had been a trickle of sightseers was now a stream rapidly becoming a flood. The deluge of ghouls passed our gate, entered the cane field, stayed for a short time, and departed. As twilight descended, the crowd thinned out, leaving only a few hardy stragglers. It was about this time that the police returned for their fourth visit.

With the arrival of a new day, I thought the people's morbid curiosity would be sated. I also expected the police to remove the body for burial. I was sadly mistaken.

Crowds continued trudging up the hill. The police sped up the hill for the fifth time, accomplishing nothing. From the complete lack of interest displayed by the public and the police, obviously the authorities hoped the body would quietly rot away.

By the third day, the stream of morbid curiosity seekers no longer trudged up the hill to stare at the corpse, not even the police. That attitude did not help us. It was disgusting. He might be dead, but he was someone's son, brother, or father. It became obvious that the police didn't want to investigate the death.

Not everyone was as heartless as the police. Shirley, who owned a nearby shop, decided to do something about the disgraceful behaviour of the Lucea authorities. She phoned a popular talk show, explaining to the host how shamefully the local authorities had behaved, especially the police. These talk shows have a great deal of influence in Jamaica. Everyone from the Prime Minister's office to the vendor selling sky juice tunes into one or more of the talk shows.

When the moderator heard Shirley's tale, he proceeded to excoriate the authorities, saying, "This is absolutely intolerable behaviour. A human being allowed to hang for days while people come and stare is unacceptable. This slackness gives Jamaica a bad reputation. Mr. Prime Minister, Mr. Superintendent of Police, how can you allow this insult to human dignity to continue for four days? Do your detachments keep you up to date on what is occurring in their area? Don't you care? Get on the phone, or better yet, go there and make sure they deal with the problem. Today! Not tomorrow! Not the next day! Today! In the future, you must do better. All Jamaicans, whether living or dead, deserve respect from those in authority. I do not want to hear that this problem continues into tomorrow. Who is our next caller?"

Not long after the end of the call-in show, Baby Lou exclaimed, "Oy, Cool. Dem comin' up the hill."

"Who coming?"

"A police Jeep, a car, and the garbage truck. Dem all stop at the cane patch," she replied.

"Do ya think they'll do something this time or just look and go away, like before?"

"Don't know, but dem all goin' in de patch. Somethin goin' on. De man in de car is no police boy. Him in a suit and tie, no police uniform."

"Maybe he's the Jamaican coroner. Baby Lou! What is that disgusting stench? It's like an ocean of shit flowing over and engulfing us. It feels like the gut-churning stench is invading my lungs. I can barely catch my breath. I feel like I'm gonna throw up. In my entire life, I have never smelt anything as nauseating."

"Dem dragging da body ta the garbage truck. Dem cut down the man. He burst when he fell. That made the terrible tink. Me rass! Dem throwin' the body inta the garbage truck."

Disgustedly, I mumbled to Baby Lou, "So much for dignity. They didn't even find out who he was or where he came from."

Was putting up with hurricane, fire, shakedown, and corpses hanging in trees for days worth it? After coming to Jamaica for the last five years, staying three months twice each year, I had still not found that elusive something. What had been adventures in the past were quickly becoming stressful problems.

The biggest problem was Baby Lou's alcoholism. Whenever she got drunk, she became belligerent, accusing me for no reason of cheating with other women. More and more, the point of contention became marriage and alcoholism.

"Marry me. We be together fi years. Why not marry me?"

"I told you. If you quit drinking, I'll marry you. Marriages where one partner is an alcoholic don't last. If they do last, there's nothing but misery."

"Marry me and me quit drinkin'. Me have a reason ta quit."

"No. Quit first, then marriage. I want to know you can do without the drink before the marriage. I don't know how much longer I can take your drunken abuse."

If I couldn't find the peace of mind I was looking for in Jamaica, then why put up with the abuse? If things didn't improve on the next trip, in January, it would be my last trip.

19
Falling in Love

January of 1992 found me in Jamaica once again, staying at Baby Lou's house.

On the cab ride to Lucea, I couldn't stop thinking about Baby Lou. I didn't know what to expect.

"When I arrive," I thought, "she'll be sweet as mango pie. How long before she comes home drunk and miserable, ready to quarrel, I don't know. This unpredictability has me on edge. If things don't change on this trip, it may well be the last."

I had no problem directing the driver to Baby Lou's house. After so many journeys, I had the route memorized.

"Oy, Baby Lou!" I called out after stopping at the gate.

When I reached the veranda, Baby Lou surprised me, saying, "Me got someone stayin' with me. When ya gone, I went to Buckup ta visit Gertie, a longtime friend. We go to Downs to see her niece. Me ask Gillette if she want to come to Lucea to visit. She say yes. She wanted a change of scenery."

"Hello, Gillette. I'm pleased to meet you."

"It's nice to meet you, sir."

"Forget the sir. Call me John."

"Yes, John."

"Gillette been wit me fa two weeks. She can keep ya company while me in town."

An extra pair of hands made the morning chores fly by. This left Baby Lou free to leave for Lucea by midmorning. Most times, she returned in the late afternoon, a little tipsy, just in time to make supper.

With Baby Lou away from the house more than usual, Gillette and I spent a great deal of time getting to know each other.

"How do you like staying with Baby Lou?"

"It be all right, but too much drinking. Every night, when ya gone, she be at the bar. She had me follow her, introducing me to all the men. I felt like she was selling me."

"That's how Baby Lou relates to men," I told Gillette. "As a child, someone molested Baby Lou, leading her into a sport life. Having lived that lifestyle, she doesn't understand how to relate to men as friends. They're a means of obtaining what she wants with sex. She could never imagine a friendship with a man that didn't involve sex."

"But I'm not like that. I don't drink, and the only time I smoked, I got sick."

"I hear a taxi. She must be coming home."

"I'll help her with the bags."

"What ya doin' when me gone?" Baby Lou demaded. "Are ya sneakin' around behind me back? Put that in de kitchen."

"Lou, nothing's going on. Now that Gillette is here, you're gone for most of the day. All we do is chat. You just can't imagine making friends without sex involved. If you're so worried about what we do, stay home. But you can't stay away from the drink."

"Top the noise. Me make supper. Gillette, peel da breadfruit."

On another occasion, when Baby Lou was in town, I asked, "Is Gillette your given name?"

"No. My name is Gillian, but people call me Gillette, Julie, Jewl, and Juliette."

"I think Gillian is a pretty name. If it's all right with you, I'll start calling you Gillian."

"Yes, I would like that."

"Why do you wash your clothes so often?"

"I only have two skirts and three blouses."

"Baby Lou has a dresser full of clothes. She could give you something to wear."

"She offered me a dress, but ya can see through the material. Her skirts are too short for me. I want a skirt just above the knee, not unda me butt. When I have money, I buy material and have a seamstress make a blouse and skirt."

"I'm sorry Baby Lou has nothing modest enough for you. Here's some money for some material. Have some new clothes made. I think I hear the cab."

"Thank you, John. Me help Baby Lou wid the baskets."

The first words out of Baby Lou's mouth, as she stepped onto the veranda were, "Me know somethin' a goin' on when me gone."

"Well, stay home," I told her, "and you'll see nothing going on except conversation."

"Me know ya doin' somethin'. Me feel it when me downtown."

"You don't feel a damn thing! There's no use talking with you. You'll only believe what you want to believe, and that's always the worst!"

I didn't know what to expect from day to day. One minute Baby Lou was cursing me for having sex with Gillian, and the next moment she was all smiles and jokes. When she behaved with decorum, she was a pleasure to be around, but when she was drunk and belligerent, I wanted nothing to do with her. Her constant accusations were beginning to irritate me. Not knowing how she would react from moment to moment kept me walking on eggshells.

On another occasion, while we whiled away another hot afternoon, I asked Gillian, "Where do you live?"

"I live at my dad's house, near Downs."

"Where's Downs? How do you get there?"

"Go to Savanna la Mar. Take the road to Kingston. Ya drive through Santa Cruz, turning right when ya reach Gutters. Ya go through Buckup and Prospect. When ya reach Downs Square, turn right toward Junction. Turn right onto the road just before the Seventh Day Adventist Church. We be the first lane after da church."

"Do you have a phone?"

"No. Me must go to the call box in Junction Square."

"What about sending a letter? Where would I send it?"

"Ya send it to Gillian White, Downs District, Watson Hill P.O., Manchester, Jamaica, W.I."

"I think I hear a taxi," I said then. "Baby Lou must be coming home. I hope she's not drunk and miserable this time."

More and more, I found myself comparing Gillian's demure, courteous demeanor with Baby Lou's increasingly quarrelsome behaviour, and Baby Lou was coming out a distant second.

Gillian's personality was delightful, but her attitude toward me was the most appealing. She accepted me as I was. My disabilities were of no great concern to her. She never made me feel like a burden. Slowly, ever so slowly, I was falling in love with her.

One evening, a few weeks after I had arrived, Baby Lou announced, "Me going ta Pym Pym's wake. She was kilt in a minibus crash."

"Remember when you went to Ivan's wake?" I asked. "Someone came to rob me. Thank God the neighbors came running with machetes when I screamed 'thief.'"

"No problem this time. Gillette will stay with ya."

With that, Baby Lou was off in a swirl in her filmy purple dress.

Lying in bed listening to my book player, I called to Gillian, "What are you watching?"

"Sonny Spoon."

"I'm lonely. Can I come over there to chat?"

"Yes!"

Wheeling to the bedroom door, I lowered myself to the floor, crawling to where I could pull myself onto the bed Gillian shared with Baby Lou.

"What a beautiful evening," I said. "Especially after the hot, sticky day. The gentle, cooling breezes wafting through the windows make everything feel dreamy. Being so close to you, I feel romantic."

Sliding my arm around Gillian's shoulders, I tentatively placed a kiss on her cheek. She didn't pull away. Instead, she turned to me. We shared a deep kiss filled with promise. Speech became superfluous, and instinct took over. We made love. Having sated ourselves, we cuddled, whispering of our love.

"Gillian, this is the most fantastic night of my life. I'll remember and cherish every minute as long as I live. I'm falling in love with you."

"What about Baby Lou? What are ya gonna tell her?"

"I don't know. All I know is that I'm in love with you. I never felt this way with Baby Lou. We had sex, but the love I feel for you was not there with Baby Lou. She considered me her boyfriend, but she didn't act the role. She could never restrict her sexual favours to one special man. Our relationship was one more of convenience than love."

Finally, I had found a woman who accepted me as a lover with no reservations.

"What can we do?" Gillian asked. "I cannot stay and put up with Baby Lou's abuse. Me must go back to Downs."

"Could we get a place In Mandeville?"

"Me can look, but it will take time."

Before I returned to my room, we held each other tight, sharing a long, lingering kiss. Back in my room, contented after making love, I was soon sound asleep.

"What the hell!" I exclaimed, as pounding on the door jerked me from sleep.

"It's me! Let me in!"

After unlocking the door, I returned to bed, followed by an angry, drunken Baby Lou. Staggering behind me, she commenced spewing out her spiteful anger. "I know ya fucked the bitch. Soon as me back turned, ya and her at it. I can smell her on ya. Somethin' told me ta come home early."

As Baby Lou ranted, I mentally ran through my options. "She's drunk," I thought, "so she wants a quarrel. If I tell her the truth, she'll quarrel. If I lie, she'll quarrel. Can't win. Tell a lie and deny, deny, deny. At least she can't say, 'I knew ya did it.'"

"Nothing happened, Lou. You always want to think the worst."

"Me know what me know. Me deal with it in de morning."

The tension the next morning was so thick you could cut it with a knife. No one spoke. While Baby Lou banged the dishes around making breakfast, Gillian packed. The stress and anger had my guts churning. I could barely choke down breakfast. Not wanting anything from Baby Lou, Gillian refused breakfast, departing for the Lucea bus stop.

For the next week, my thoughts were preoccupied with Gillian. How was she? Did she arrive safely? And the big question: How would I get to see her again?

20
Gillian

For weeks after her departure, the need to see Gillian consumed me. I had to see her again, but how? If I took the mini bus, I needed Merrick to accompany me to help with the wheelchair. I would have to catch three separate buses to get to Downs. Having to wait for each bus and return would take an entire day. In addition, it would be impossible for me to go on the bus without Baby Lou finding out and making my life a living hell. I needed to find a ride that Baby Lou could never trace. To accomplish that, I needed to talk with someone with a car, and the only one I knew was Speedy, Baby Lou's brother.

"Speedy, do you know how I can get to Downs to visit Gillian? I need a ride, and I can't take a taxi, because eventually, the driver will mention it to someone. Soon everyone will know, and some spiteful person will mention it to Baby Lou."

"Me take ya, but it be a long trip. If me gone long, me have ta tell Heikie. Me don't want her ta think me cheatin' or there will be pure trouble. If she know, she will tell Baby Lou."

"I can't have that happen. I'd never hear the end."

"Me got an idea. Me brethren Justice may take ya. Give him

gas money and somethin' fa drivin' ya."

One afternoon, when Baby Lou was in Lucea, Speedy dropped by with Justice for a chat.

"Speedy mentioned you might be willing to drive me to Downs to see Gillian," I said. "I understand it's a long trip. I'll fill up your tank before and after the journey and give you something for driving me. I need to talk with her."

"Ya, mun, I can drive ya, but not fi a few days. Da car need some work. Me tell Speedy when me can come fi ya."

A few days later, Justice arrived in his red and green Triumph convertible. I would be riding in style on the journey to Gillian's house. However, until I sat on the seat, I didn't appreciate how small his car was. It couldn't even accommodate the wheelchair in the trunk.

Usually on a trip, I was a chatterbox. "Where are we? What do you see? How much longer?" Not this time. Thoughts of Gillian preoccupied me. Would she be home? Would she still feel the same toward me? Not long, and I would know.

Anticipation made the miles fly past. Before I knew it, Justice stopped at a shop, inquiring, "Da ya know where Gillette White lives?"

Pointing, the shop owner said, "Take dat road. Turn left at the first lane, and ya at da house."

Parking in Gillian's lane, Justice went to a nearby shop, leaving Gillian and me alone.

Pulling Gillian close to me, I gave her the biggest hug ever, whispering, "I missed you so much. Every day, I think of you. Now that I've met you, I'm only happy when I'm with you. Every day away is torture."

"I, too, miss ya. I wish we could be together all de time, but I don't know how. I can't find a place for us ta stay."

"If I could just hear your voice every day, I would be happy.

It can't happen with no phone. All we can do is write letters, which is of no use to me. Separation from you is so frustrating. Unable to make our life better, I feel useless. We could meet in Negril, but I don't know how to get in touch with you without a phone."

"Ya must come to Downs to take me ta Negril."

All too soon, our time was up. I had to return to Lucea.

"I'll miss you so much," I told her.

"Me too. Gi me one kiss before ya go."

One last hug, a lingering kiss, and it was time to depart. Having visited with Gillian, I had nothing to look forward to on the return trip. In fact, I dreaded returning to Baby Lou, not knowing what was in store for me when I arrived.

Around Easter, my brother Frank and his wife, Linda, stopped at the house in Lucea to visit on their way to Negril.

"Things have sure changed!" Frank exclaimed. "You had nothing when I was last here. Now you have electricity, color television, a fan, and a fridge. You're stepping up in the world."

"I still wish we had a phone and running water," I said. "I can get a hot shower with the solar water bag, but getting the water for the bag is still the problem. How long will you be in Negril?"

"We're only here for a week. We couldn't get more time off."

"I want to visit you and Linda for a couple of days. I think I can catch a ride with Bunga to Negril. Where will you stay?"

"We'll stay at Tigress Two."

"With luck, I'll meet you there in a couple of days."

The prospect of visiting Frank and Linda in Negril had me excited. I could hardly wait to tell them all about Gillian. How could I arrange for her to meet them?

A few days later, I caught a ride to Negril with Bunga Ray, Arriving at Tigress Two in the mid-morning.

Catching Frank and Linda as they finished their breakfast of sausage and eggs, I was bursting to tell them my news. "Frank, Linda, I'm in love. I've met the most wonderful woman in the world. When you get to meet her, you'll see what a fantastic person she is."

"With hype like that, I can't wait to meet her. When will we get to see her?"

"I don't know what to do. She has no phone, so I can't call. All I can do is get a taxi to Downs and hope she's home."

For the remainder of the day, whenever we were out, I asked drivers, "How much to take me to Downs?"

Some answered, "Me don't know where dat be." Others refused, saying, "Me don't leave Negril. Me car ta old."

Returning to Tigress after supper, I chanced on some tourists exiting a minibus. Wheeling to the driver, I asked, "Hey, brother, do ya know the way to Downs?"

"Ya, mun. Me brethren got people in Junction."

"How much there and back?"

"A hundred and fifty U.S."

"Too much. I'll give you a hundred Canadian."

Turning to one of his brethren, he asked, "Do ya know the short way ta Downs?"

"Ya, mun."

"No problem. We'll take ya for a hundred Canadian."

"Frank, can you lend me a hundred?"

"Sure, here. I also want the license plate number and their names in case you don't return."

Once again, I was off on an adventure with three complete strangers.

My traveling companions kept up a lively conversation, but I didn't partake. Thoughts of Gillian and the journey preoccupied me.

"I'm traveling on back roads with three strangers," I thought. "Will I make it back alive? Don't give it a second thought, John. There's nothing you can do. Enjoy the ride."

I still couldn't enjoy the trip. All I could thing about was Gillian. "Will she be home? What can I do if she's not home? Please, please be home!"

As we closed in on our destination, my anticipation increased.

"She must be home!" I thought. "I'll soon be with Gillian. I need Frank and Linda to meet her."

Finally, when I was about to burst, we rolled into Gillian's yard, whereupon I yelled out, "Gillian! Are you home?"

To my great relief, I heard an answering cry. "John! What a surprise!"

When Gillian reached the mini bus, I asked, "Do you want to go to Negril? I have some people I want you to meet."

"Yes, mun! Me soon come. Me pack a bag."

Heaving a huge sigh of relief, I relaxed, chatting with my traveling companions until Gillian stepped into the van. With Gillian beside me, the ride to Negril flew by. Thoughts of introducing Gillian to Frank and Linda had me eager.

After stowing her bag in the room, we were off to meet them.

"Gillian, I'd like you to meet my brother, Frank, and his wife, Linda."

"Hello, Gillian. We're glad to meet you."

"Thank you. I'm also happy to meet ya."

"Ever since we arrived, John hasn't been able to stop talking about you."

"I hope he told you good things."

"I could never say anything bad about you," I told her. "Meeting you is the best thing that ever happened to me."

"It's obvious that you're both in love," Frank said.

When Frank and I were alone, he commented, "You met a wonderful woman. She appears to love you despite the blindness and paralysis. I've never met another woman that treated you so well. You've struck gold."

"You are so right. Separation from Gillian leaves me with an empty feeling in the pit of my stomach."

"Sure enough. You're in love."

Before Gillian returned to Downs, I told her my plans. "I'll leave for Canada in a couple of weeks. When I'm back in Canada, you can call me from the call box in Junction. This isn't ideal, but it's the best I can do given the circumstances."

Back in Canada, I anxiously awaited calls from Gillian. With each new day, I anticipated a call. When Mom called out, "John, call from Jamaica," I was ecstatic. When I came home after being out and Mom said, "You just missed a call from Jamaica," I was heartbroken.

On one of our last phone calls, I arranged to meet Gillian in Negril before going to Lucea and Baby Lou. On this trip, Ragamuffin Bob accompanied me. He was dying to meet Gillian.

"Bob, this is Gillian. Gillian, this is Ragamuffin Bob."

"Greetings, Ragamuffin Bob. Glad to meet ya."

"Pleased to meet you also, Gillian. So you are the wonderful woman John can't stop talking about. It's Gillian this, Gillian that. The man is in love."

After a couple of days together, Gillian returned to Downs, and Bob and I returned to Lucea and Baby Lou. Before separating, Gillian and I arranged another rendezvous for a few weeks later at Lily Mae's Cozy Inn.

On the ride to Lucea, Bob raved, "She's a keeper. I don't know how a miserable old goat like you met such a good woman. You don't deserve her. She must be the blind one. Congratulations."

When Bob Volpe, my roommate from Canada, visited me in Jamaica, I arranged for us to go to Negril. I wanted him to meet Gillian. As with everyone else, her kind, cheery demeanor immediately enthralled him

"You're lucky to find someone like Gillian," Bob said to me. "Gillian, I don't know what you see in him. He must be working some powerful Obeah on you."

Before departing for Canada this time, I gave Gillian some money, saying, "I'm tired of running up and down in order to be with you. What we spend on rooms and taxis will pay for rent. We need our own place. You must be able to find something in Mandeville."

"Me ask people I know in Mandeville. If there be a place to rent, dem will know."

"I hope you have good luck. I'm looking forward to spending my entire time with you on the next trip. Phone me as soon as you have a place, so I know where to go when I land."

After a couple of months in Canada, Gillian had still not found lodgings for us. I was beginning to lose hope when I heard "John, phone call."

"Hello, Gillian."

"John! Me find a place in Mandeville! It be easy to move around with the wheelchair."

"Fantastic! I can't wait. We'll be together for the entire trip. And I have a surprise for you."

"What is it?"

"It's a surprise. I can't tell you. I have to show you."

Landing in Kingston, I wasted no time getting a taxi to

Mandeville. Reaching Mandeville, the driver stopped a couple of times to get directions to the Myers place.

Stopping at a gate, the driver inquired, "Do ya be Mr. Myers?"

"Yes, mun."

"Do ya have a Gillian White living here?"

Before Mr. Myers could reply, Gillian ran out yelling, "Hi, John! Me home. I'm so happy to see ya. Squeeze me tight."

Pushing me into the new apartment, Gillian was bursting with excitement at the thought of showing me our new home. "This is the hall. Over here is the bed and dresser. There are some chairs. This be the bathroom. There be a tub, toilet, and sink, but no running water. Me bring water from the tank in da yard. This little room be the kitchen. Me use a gas stove and kerosene lamps. No current."

"That doesn't matter. All that matters is that we're together. We don't have to hide anymore."

Within a couple of days, I felt completely at home. "Gillian, living like this, we're almost married. Would you like to marry me?"

"Oh, yes! I hoped ya would ask."

Slipping the ring on her finger, I again asked, "Are you sure you can put up with me forever?"

"Yes! I love you, and I want to share your life forever."

"What do we have to do to get married?" I asked.

"I don't know. Me ask at the Adventist church in Downs."

Upon gleaning the information we needed, Gillian told me, "Them tell me they must interview us, and we must go to a six-month marriage course."

"That's not going to happen. I can only stay for three months at a time. It will take a year before we marry. I hope to start the paperwork for immigration when I return to Canada."

"Me ask some friends what to do."

After questioning various friends, Gillian finally arrived at a plan. "Me find a J.P. willing to marry us. He is also a pastor at the Jehovah's Witnesses church. He will perform the service on Saturday, November 13, at 11:00."

"Who will we get for witnesses?"

"Sharon, my niece, will be my maid of honor."

"I'll get Merrick for my best man. I would get Bunga Ray, but Rastas don't deal with Christian rituals. Merrick is a great friend. He helped me accomplish so many things. He's become my closest friend in Jamaica."

Eating an early breakfast, we showered and dressed for the special day. I didn't have a suit, so I made do with gray dress pants and a short-sleeved white shirt. Gillian wore a new sky-blue dress with flower embroidery. Shortly after we finished dressing, Sharon arrived from Downs. Merrick was the last to arrive. He had been lucky enough to catch a ride with Bunga Ray on his way to Kingston.

I will never forget November 13, 1993. On that day, God smiled on us, granting us a magnificent, sunny, 84-degree day for our wedding. With everyone present on this beautiful day, Merrick flagged down a taxi for our ride to destiny.

Since the J.P. was also a pastor, he delivered a homily on marriage before performing the marriage ceremony.

"Gillian and John, you are about to embark on the most momentous step of your lives. When you leave here, you will no longer be two separate individuals pursuing your separate goals. You will be one, sharing all that befalls you. I want you to take a minute to meditate on the implications that this step involves. This is forever. I have seen many marriages fail because the people rushed into them. Be certain. Are you certain you want to take this step?"

"Yes!" I stated emphatically.

"Yes!" Gillian unhesitatingly answered.

"Since you are both certain, I will proceed with the ceremony. Do you, Gillian Sharon White, take John Walter Cronin to be your lawfully wedded husband, for better or worse, in sickness and in health, for richer or poorer, forsaking all others, until death do you part?"

"I do!"

"Now, do you, John Walter Cronin, take Gillian Sharon White to be your lawfully wedded wife, for better or worse, in sickness and in health, for richer or poorer, forsaking all others, until death do you part?"

"I do."

"I pronounce you man and wife. You may kiss the bride."

We kissed, and he said, "It's time to sign the papers. John, Gillian, you sign here and here. Winsome and Dwart, you sign here. You have signed, I have affixed my seal, and I will deliver the one copy to the registry in Kingston. Here is your copy. I hope you have a long, happy life together."

We didn't have much time together. If I didn't want to get in trouble with immigration, I had to leave in two weeks.

For this trip, Bunga Ray drove us from Mandeville to a hotel in Montego Bay. The next morning, Gillian helped me pack the oil before we departed for the airport.

"I'll miss you so much, Gillian. Every day away from you is torture. I'll be back as soon as possible."

"I love you, John. Come back quick. Me miss ya so much. Give me one last kiss."

21
Robbery

Although I occasionally spoke with Gillian, time still dragged by. I couldn't stop thinking about her. What was she doing? Did she miss me? Was she safe? The only way to answer my questions was reunification with her.

The day before I departed, a blizzard dumped a foot of snow on southern Ontario, grounding all flights. I tossed and turned all night, hoping the weather would clear for the next day. The next morning, I woke to blue skies and a bright, sunny day. My flight was only half an hour late. I felt like I was going home.

On the ride from Kingston to Mandeville, my thoughts were of Gillian. I could hardly wait to hold her. Now we were man and wife.

Reaching the Myers' gate, I was about to yell for Gillian when Mr. Myers stepped up to the minivan. "Gillian not be here. She move a few days ago. She be at her father's house in Downs."

I was dumbfounded. I managed to stammer out, "What happened? Why did she move?"

"A tief kicked in da door and robbed her. Me got no money ta fix da door, so she went ta Downs."

I was speechless. Finally, when the surprise wore off, I told the driver, "I guess we're going to Downs."

"How do I get there?"

Still stunned by the news, I managed to mumble, "No problem; I can direct you."

Not receiving much information from Myers allowed my imagination to run rampant. The ride to Downs seemed to take forever, and I was bursting with unanswered questions. Was Gillian injured? Is she still frightened? What did the thief take? Did they catch him?

When I arrived, Gillian embraced me, squeezing so hard I thought I might burst.

"Me so glad ya here. Me did not think about ya coming when I run from Myers. All me could think of was getting away."

"None of that matters. When Mr. Myers told me you left, I thought the worst. Did the thief harm you? Did they catch him?"

"Slow down, John. I'll tell ya what happened. I heard a knocking on the burglar-barred window. Going to the window, I asked, 'Who do ya want?'

"'You' was his reply.

"'No, because I don't know ya.'

"Some people did move in around back of the house that same week, so I said, 'Maybe ya need those people dat just move in around back.'

"He said, 'No! Me want ya!'

"'But I don't know ya.'

"So I walk away, and then I heard the door being kicked. I started to yell, and he came in! When he came in, the first thing he ask me for was me jewelry. I said, 'I don't have any jewelry.' He said he saw me with them. And then he was arguing with me.

I told him, 'Well, if you want them, go look for them. Go find them yourself.'

"Then him walk up into the front room, and I slip out through the back door. After a while, when my friends they came home from a party, they find me standing out there in the road. And they ask me, 'What's the matter?'

"I tell them, 'There is a guy came kick my door in, and he is inside the house.'

"So they take me to the police station. When I come back with the police, he's already gone. So the things I lost, it was my jewelry and few dollars in the drawer. So he took the money, too."

I asked, "Did they find him?"

"No, the police did not find the guy. But he go to another girl's house next door and he do the same thing like what he do with me. So he go around that night to places him spotted out with woman and no man. But the girl had a boyfriend. When him return from Kingston, he saw the thief on a road and stab him in the belly. Dem thief end up at the hospital. But he already has a bad record with the police that take him in. When that happen, well, the doctor don't pay you too much attention. So he just stay there, suffer, and die."

"Wow! What a story! I'm so glad you weren't injured, Gillian. I worry about you."

"Don't worry. It'll do no good."

Now that I had heard Gillian's tale of terror, I had to become acquainted with my new relatives and surroundings. Like all my previous abodes, this house had no running water, telephone, or electricity. The house was a cement block structure with three bedrooms, a bathing room, a hall, and a veranda. The kitchen was a small room on the outside of the house. Gillian and I shared one bedroom, while her niece

Monique and great-niece, Tally, occupied the other bedroom. Her brothers, Hector and Danny, shared the third bedroom.

Since the bathing room had no toilet, Gillian arranged an alternative. She had part of a chair seat removed and a bucket with water placed under it.

This was the first time while in Jamaica that I dealt with so many people on a daily basis. Along with the immediate family members, two more nieces, Sharon and Simone, were frequent visitors. Nearby cousins and friends dropped in regularly.

"Gillian," I told her, "being the new member of the family, I feel like an outsider. I have no friends except you. Everyone has known everyone else forever. They have no incentive to go out of their way to befriend me. I have less time with you because you have so many other people making demands on your time. At times, I just feel so sad and lonely."

"Me sorry, but me don't know what ta do. Everyone pulling me this way and that. Not good, living with so many people."

Then and there, I decided to do whatever I needed to do to get along. This was only temporary. Gradually, with help from Gillian, I began to form friendships. Just as I became more comfortable with the people and surroundings, my three months' stay was at an end. Leaving Gillian was becoming more and more difficult.

This time, my departure took a different turn. I had to go to Lucea to talk with Jimmy, the Rasta that made the oil. To accomplish this, Bunga picked me up in Downs and took me to Lucea. I didn't like doing this because I lied, telling Baby Lou, "I just arrived. I can only stay for ten days this time. I have to keep my eye on a guy back home. He owes me money. If I don't keep reminding him, he forgets."

"What about you sexing me? Ya always want it. Why not now?"

"Not this time. I'm seeing the doctor about my prostate problem."

When I saw Jimmy, I told him, "People complained about the last batch. I hope this batch is better."

"Ya, mun. Try it. It be good."

Using a matchstick, I spread some oil on a cigarette paper, sprinkled in some tobacco, and sparked up the spliff.

"You're right. The oil tastes good."

Handing me a watch, Jimmy said, "Here, mun. Can ya get ma Rolex fixed?"

Taking the gold Rolex from Jimmy, I said, "No problem. I'll get it repaired it and return it when I come back. You can pay me in oil. Later, man."

"Cool runnings. Safe trip, mun."

22
Busted

With things arranged to my satisfaction and everything packed, I climbed aboard the minibus for the ride to the airport.

During the ride, I felt nervous. Driving along the twisting road to Montego Bay, I thought, "The omens are against me. A blizzard almost canceled my flight. Gillian moved because someone broke into her apartment and robbed her. Last but not least, I had problems with Jimmy over the oil. Is this trip cursed? I'd better shake off this foolishness before I get to the airport."

The check-in went smoothly, but I still couldn't shake the uneasy feeling. When I reached the security gate, nothing seemed amiss. As always, the security guards pulled me from the line in order to frisk me. They couldn't use a metal detector on me because of all the metal around and inside me.

The security guard said, "Sir, I have to physically search you since you cannot go through the metal detector. Could you please extend your arms to the side?"

Having finished sliding his rubber-gloved hands along my arms and legs, he asked, "Sir, could you lean forward?"

Leaning forward, I felt his hands slide down my back,

slipping between my back and the padded pelvic girdle of my leg braces. By now, my shirt was soaked with sweat. Fear had me shaking like a leaf in a storm.

"Jackpot! They got the honey oil taped to the girdle," I thought. "Now what?"

Sniggering, the guard asked, "What is this, sir? Come with me! We will need to investigate this further."

He wheeled me through a nearby door.

When we entered the security room, the guards hoisted me out of the wheelchair, laying me on a cold metal table. They quickly pulled down my pants, revealing the oil strapped to the undersides of my thighs. Rolling me over, they revealed the package taped to the pelvic girdle, allowing them to cut it free.

Having found and removed the three packages of oil, they allowed me to dress and return to the wheelchair, where I sat in stunned silence. Everything had moved so swiftly that there was no time for me to fully comprehend what had happened.

The next thing I knew, a woman addressed me, saying, "Hello, Mr. Cronin. I'm here as a representative of the Canadian consulate here in Montego Bay. We're here to aid Canadian citizens when they come into conflict with Jamaican law. I'm sorry we're meeting under these circumstances, but I'll do everything in my power to assist you."

"What's going to happen?" I mumbled, hanging my head in humiliation. "How can you help me? You can't get me out of this jam. Or can you?"

"No, Mr. Cronin, I can't solve the problem. As to your first question, the police will transport you from here to a holding cell. Tomorrow you go before a judge for arraignment. What I can do for you is arrange for a lawyer. Other Canadians have used this lawyer when they encountered problems. You'll be responsible for any agreement you make with him concerning payment. I can also make any calls to Canada to notify people of your dilemma."

"Thank you." I almost wept. "Could you phone Bob, my roommate? He can tell anyone who needs to know."

The representative prepared to depart. The only person who had shown me any compassion in the last half hour was about to leave. I was frightened.

After her departure, the police pushed me outside, into the blistering hot sun. When we reached the vehicle, one of the guards towering over me ordered, "Go inna de car, bwoy. Just cause ya crippled, ya tink ya gonna get betta treatment from me. Ya just extra work, bwoy. I gotta put this blasted chair in da back of the car."

Sliding into the back seat of the car, I found myself surrounded by police. There were two up front and one on either side of me. They wanted to ensure that the blind paraplegic did not make a break for freedom.

On the ride to the holding cells, I had time to reflect on all the horror stories I had heard about third-world jails. These thoughts stoked my already mounting fear. I couldn't control my shaking. The stories the guards reveled in telling me only intensified my dread.

"Ay, bwoy. Them big Black bwoys is gonna enjoy your white ass. None of dem like white bwoys. They's just waiting to get dem hands on ya."

By now, visions of big Black men sodomizing me possessed my thoughts. I could do nothing but hope that my incarceration would not be as brutal as the guards said it would be. All I could do was to be easygoing and friendly and hope for the best

When we reached the main lockup, my guard turned to me, laughing, "Can you hear all dem animals yelling? Dem jus waitin' ta get dem hands on ya, bwoy. Thems hungerin' for ya."

A cacophony of prisoners yelling and rattling and banging bars greeted me as I lifted myself from the police car to the wheelchair.

While shaking the iron bars of their cages, the prisoners yelled out, "Ay, white bwoy! Gimme some money! Come now, mun. Me hungry. You'll see what it's like."

Having wheeled past the gauntlet of yelling, banging prisoners, I arrived at the prison office.

"Oy, who we got here?" the sergeant inquired.

"We picked up da boy at the airport. Another fool. Here's da passport," the officer replied, handing over my passport.

While they processed me, I remained as quiet as a mouse. I hoped to glean some information about my future. I learned nothing. All I heard were grumblings from the guards about shifting prisoners to make room for a wheelchair. The way they carried on, I assumed I was the first wheelchair guest at their iron-bar hotel. With the paperwork completed, they pushed me to the cage.

Clang, bang, as the first gate was unlocked and relocked. I was now in the holding area. More keys jangled and a gate clanged, locking me into my new home.

Immediately, a clamour of greetings and questions assaulted me.

"Welcome, man. How are you, man? Where ya from? What you in for?"

Instantaneously, it hit me. I heard various voices, but none spoke with a Jamaican accent. I was not in a cell with angry Black men. My companions' accents seemed familiar.

With my confidence returning, I replied, "I'm from Canada. What about everyone else?"

"Me too! I'm from Toronto," someone piped up.

A French accent chimed in. "I'm from Montreal."

Not wanting to be left out, another added, "I'm from Kingston. I used to live in Jamaica, but now I'm a Canadian."

"Wow," was all I could blurt out. "Is everyone from Canada?"

Toronto replied, "The two guys on the top bunk are Dutch. They don't speak English. My friend here is from Colombia, and I think we have a couple of boys from the good old U.S. of A. We are truly an international collection of desperadoes. What ya in for?"

"They caught me with some oil."

Toronto laughed. "Don't sweat, it brother. We're all in here for drugs. The cops popped everyone at the airport. I guess you got caught there, too."

"Yes. They grabbed three elbows of honey oil from me."

Jumping down from the bunk, Toronto clasped my hand, saying, "You missed supper. No loss. All they give us is chicken back and boiled dumplings. They're so big, people call them cartwheels. If you got money, you can order out. We just finished some KFC. We pooled some money and got the turnkey to bring us some edible grub. That's him sitting in the holding area just outside our cell."

I was astonished. "These people are prisoners," I thought, "but the turnkey brings whatever they want. How far will he go? I guess I'll find out."

I soon had an inkling of how far the delivery service went when Toronto offered me a beer, saying, "Have a Red Stripe. It's not cold. The one thing we're missing is ice. A spliff would sure go good with the beer, but we're out. Do you have any?"

Wanting to endear myself to my new friends, I piped up, "No problem!" Reaching into the front of my pants, I extracted an ounce of compressed marijuana. "The bastards missed this." With a smile, I handed the package to Toronto, saying, "Enjoy, brothers!"

All we needed were rolling papers. This was no problem. Some money changed hands with the turnkey, and rolling papers magically appeared. Soon the cage was filling with marijuana smoke. The turnkey even had a couple of draws from the spliff as it made the rounds.

Someone else produced some money for a couple of beers so we could quench our parched throats. It was not long before the cage was alive with our singing and talking. My first time in jail was quickly turning into a party.

A beer, a joint, and my new friends worked their magic. The stress and anxiety building over the last few hours slowly drained from me. A warm feeling of euphoria washed over me. With my confidence returning, I knew I could survive this disaster.

Wanting to familiarize myself with my surroundings, I asked, "What does the cell look like?"

"You're in a 10-by-10-by-10-foot concrete cube. There are three sets of concrete bunks with no mattresses. Located high on the outside wall is a small barred window that provides very little ventilation. In the corner, there's a sink with no water and a toilet with a broken seat. There's a barred gate at the front of the cell separating us from the holding area, where the turnkey stays."

It was obvious they had designed the cell for six prisoners, but it now held nine, including me. Poor ventilation and crowding turned our cell into a sweatbox. I was sweaty and thirsty, but drinking water was in short supply, and beer was a poor substitute.

With the onset of dusk, the, the turnkey called out, "John Cronin, ya gotta visitor. Come to the gate."

As I wheeled into the holding area, I wondered who could

be visiting. No one in Jamaica knew I'd been busted.

"Hello, Mr. Cronin. My name is Alton Williams. The Canadian consulate sent me to see if I could assist you with your problem. I've helped other Canadians who found themselves in similar circumstances. If you engage me, I need 2,000 Canadian dollars for my services. You also need up to 50,000 Jamaican dollars to pay any fines."

Having no alternative and wanting out of prison, I said, "I accept your conditions. Phone my wife, Gillian, at 876-546-9898. She can travel to Mandeville, get the money, and bring it to court, but it will take a lot of time on the minibus. Could you also phone Bunga Ray? If possible, he could meet Gillian in Sav and speed up her journey, so she can arrive at court by noon."

"I can do that," the lawyer replied. "Tell me the circumstances surrounding your case."

"Well, when I was in Negril, a Rasta I met talked me into buying some oil to take back to Canada. Every time I met him, he told me there would be no problem getting it home because they never check people in wheelchairs. Finally, he convinced me, so I gave him some money to buy the oil. On the day scheduled for my departure, he came to the hotel room and helped me pack the oil onto the brace. I guess he lied when he said there would be no problem."

Pondering for a short time, Alton finally said, "I think I can get you off with a fine. Explaining how he led you astray and that you feel remorse for your actions will go a long way toward placating the judge. Prior to sentencing, the judge may ask if you want to address the court. At this time, you may mention that you learned your lesson and will certainly never do this again. It will also help that keeping a person with your problems in prison would be difficult and not good public relations."

As I slowly wheeled back to the cage, I thought that maybe

this would be the one time that being a blind paraplegic was advantageous. At least I hoped so.

Back in the cell, I explained my deal with the lawyer to my new friends.

Montreal exclaimed, "He's robbing you. They're crooks. It's a big fraud. Get busted, pay a lawyer big money, and pay a big fine."

"Like Montreal said," Toronto broke in. "It's a scam to get money out of us. I'm not feeding it. I'm going to defend myself."

Listening to all this negativity, I wondered if my lawyer was trying to rip me off. All my cellmates seemed to think so. The faith I had in my lawyer was quickly waning.

Wanting to regain my confidence, I said, "But he only wants 2,000 Canadian and whatever the fine is. It's not much to get out of here. How long have you been waiting for your day in court?"

"Ten days," Montreal said.

"I've only waited five days," Toronto chimed in.

I no longer worried about the lawyer cheating me. I wanted out, and I was willing to pay.

With the arrival of night, our cell began to cool down, giving us a break from the sauna-like conditions. It was time to prepare for bed.

Being the new man, I had to make do with the floor, as the bunks all had occupants. With the two Dutchmen sharing a bunk, that left Montreal and me on the floor. Reaching under a bunk, he pulled out a couple of pieces of cardboard. This was supposed to provide us with some insulation from the cool, damp concrete floor. Lowering myself onto the cardboard, I grabbed my seat cushion, wanting it for a pillow.

Completely drained by the events of the last 10 hours, I was badly in need of sleep. However, a sound sleep was impossible under these conditions. I tried dozing, but with little success. Every time I started to drift off, an extra loud honk from one of my cellmates brought me wide awake. The cardboard provided very little protection from the unyielding concrete floor. The worst distraction was the silky touch of the roaches' feelers as they scampered around my face and hair. Whenever I felt or thought I felt their gentle touch, I wildly flailed my arms about, hoping to drive them away forever. No luck! Before long, they returned with friends.

The next morning, we awoke to the din of guards banging on the cell bars with their truncheons while cursing us. Still groggy from the lack of sleep, we staggered into the holding area to the accompaniment of banging gates and rattling chains. Assembling in the holding area, we awaited the next orders.

While we waited, the guards fed us a breakfast of sweet, lukewarm tea and stale bread. The bread was so hard, it had to be soaked in the tea to keep us from breaking our teeth on it. While we gulped tea and sucked on stale bread, the guards prepared us for transportation to court.

Before we had time to finish breakfast, the guards proceeded to put leg hobbles, handcuffs, and belly chains on us as they prepared us for the ride to the courthouse.

One particularly miserable guard decided to have some fun by trying to intimidate me. "Ay, boy. Me gonna chain ya to dat chair," he exclaimed, shaking the handcuffs and belly chains in my face. "Every day we gonna do this. Ya gonna come back from da court, and me gonna chain ya the next day. Ya not gittin' away from me. Ya nuttin' but problems, bwoy. Me can't get ya blood clot chair in the van. Dem police boys gonna have ta push ya ta court. When dem a pushin' ya down the street, everyone gonna be a pointin' and laughin' at ya. Ya's nuttin' but trouble." He grunted in disgust, pushing me from the holding area into the hot sun.

The job of pushing me to court fell to two guards. One pushed the wheelchair, while the other guard ensured I didn't escape. Transportation to court in this manner was humiliating. They forced me into a four-block perp walk. I was a spectacle, providing entertainment for the jeering crowds.

People cried out, "Ay, white boy, what ya do? Dem gonna put ya in jail. Gimme some money, boy!" "Want some of dis?" women bawled out, clutching at their private parts. Some sympathetic bystanders demanded, "Let da crippled-up white man go, ya brute! Him not hurt ya."

After what seemed like forever, we reached the foot of the courthouse steps. At last I would be able to escape the taunts and jeers of the crowd. However, at this point, I encountered another problem.

I could not believe it when the guards suggested, "Ya should give us a little sumptin' for all dis trouble. We had ta push ya four block down de road. See all da steps we gotta drag ya up? A lotta work."

"What should I do?" I thought. "Will they just abandon me if I don't pay? I have to get to court if I want out of this predicament. Make promises. Worry about keeping them later."

Hoping to placate the guards, I explained, "I got no money. They took everything when they arrested me. I could give you something when my wife arrives. Please, just get me into the courthouse."

Entering the courthouse, they ushered me into the courtroom, where I consulted my lawyer. Since Gillian had not arrived with the money, he would ask the judge to put the case off until the afternoon session. It was obvious nothing would happen until the lawyer received his pay.

Listening as the clerk called cases and the judge dispensed justice, I thought, "What if Gillian doesn't make it in time for my case to be dealt with today? If she doesn't make it, it's back to the cage and roaches for me. That would be a shitty mess, but if I must, I must. Think positive! Just because the noon recess arrived without Gillian doesn't mean she's not coming. Stop your shaking. No more negative vibes. She'll arrive. Oh, I think I hear a familiar voice. Yes! It's Gillian!"

Throwing my arms around her, I buried my face in her shoulder, crying, "I'm so glad to see you. I worried that something had happened to you on the road." With my tears of joy soaking her shoulder, I asked, "How was the trip? Did you have any problems?"

"I'll tell ya if ya calm down," Gillian said. "Last night, the lawyer called. Him tell me about the money. I call Bunga. I tell him to meet me Sav. I get up early, get de money, and catch a taxi to Sav. Bunga met me. I come sooner, but de bank did not open until nine o'clock."

With Gillian's arrival, the case could proceed. It was the first case called after the lunch recess. Addressing the judge, my lawyer explained the circumstances leading up to my arrest. He spoke of the remorse I felt for breaking Jamaican law. He stressed that I had learned my lesson and would not be a re-offender. In addition, incarceration would not serve as a deterrent and would be difficult because of my paralysis.

I received a fine of 2,000 Jamaican dollars, 100 Canadian. I thanked the judge for his leniency, promising never to break Jamaican law again. I've kept that promise.

I thought I was free to leave, but a police officer quickly shattered that illusion. The last formality consisted of fingerprinting.

The officer tasked with the job, said, "We need your prints in case you commit another crime. If ya want, I can help with de record. For a little something, the prints could disappear."

"No thanks. I won't be committing any more crimes in Jamaica."

As I answered, I thought, "This is the final kick at the can. No more chances for extortion, I hope."

Even though I completed the fingerprinting routine, I still had red tape to take care of before the nightmare finally ended. I needed to recover my carry-on bag and murse (my man-purse) from the central lockup and my suitcase from the Air Canada desk. Because of the ride given us by Bunga Ray, we were able to accomplish the tasks much faster.

Upon my arrival at the holding cells, the yelling prisoners and clanging bars did not intimidate me the way they had on my previous visit. Confidently, I presented my release papers to the chief guard. He perused the papers, handed me my carry-on bag and murse, and told me to have a good day.

Having attained my goal, I quickly departed—but not before ensuring that the $100 bill and the Rolex watch secreted in the false bottom of the murse were still there.

The next stop was the Air Canada desk. Here, I needed to produce my ticket stub, boarding pass, and passport. With everything in order, I received my bags, but not without some sniggers at my embarrassing position. Later, upon checking the bag, I found that someone had stolen my six-CD collector's edition Bob Marley box set. After the experiences of the past day, I felt like a plucked chicken.

Finally, Bunga drove us to a hotel, wishing me a better trip this time. Upon entering the room, the first thing I thought of was taking a steaming hot shower to rid myself of the prison stench.

After thoroughly soaking and scrubbing the prison stink from my body, I gave Gillian a big hug. Again, tears of joy and relief ran down my cheeks. The ordeal may have been over, but my baser needs were making themselves known. My stomach made growling noises, like a dog guarding a bone. It hadn't experienced food since the meagre breakfast the previous day. With a big meal under my belt, it was time to catch up on the sleep I didn't get the previous night. With no snores, roaches, or worry, sleep came quickly.

The next day went smoothly. I received a few stares and raised eyebrows when they found out why I had missed my flight, but there was no problem. I arrived safely back in Canada.

Note

Honey oil is a tincture made by soaking marijuana in alcohol. After a period, they strain off the marijuana, leaving only the marijuana-infused alcohol. They then apply heat, evaporating off the alcohol, leaving a thick, buckwheat-colored, oily substance. This is the honey oil.

23
Coming to Canada

After the disaster in Jamaica, it would be a long time before I returned. That meant I had to get Gillian to Canada as quickly as possible. I missed her so much.

With Mom's help, I filled out the paperwork and had documents copied and certified, enclosing a cheque for $800. Now that the application was in the mail, it was up to the government.

Every day, after Mom checked the mailbox, I asked, "Anything for me?"

"Sorry, John. Nothing this time."

At last, after a few months, she said, "Yes, John, it's for you."

"What does it say?"

"Gillian's paperwork has been passed onto the High Commission in Kingston, Jamaica. Now it's up to Gillian to get her paperwork filled out and returned to the High Commission."

Filling out the forms and having documents copied and certified was difficult in Jamaica. To expedite matters, Gillian hired Lee, a Justice of the Peace who performed this service for numerous others in the community. Lee was supposed to fill out the paperwork, certify all documents, and take the completed, signed forms to the High Commission in Kingston, all for one price.

As months passed with no notification from Canadian immigration, I started to wonder what was amiss. Phoning my MP's office, I asked someone to make inquiries at immigration.

Shortly after, I received a call from a representative from immigration who told me, "The paperwork for Mrs. Cronin was sent six months ago. If the papers are not completed and returned in two months, you will have to resubmit the application. I encourage Mrs. Cronin to complete the forms as quickly as possible and submit them."

I was stunned. What the hell had happened? Why weren't the forms filled out and at the High Commission? Someone had badly screwed up.

Grabbing the phone, I dialed Gillian's number. "Hello, Gillian. What's happening with your paperwork? I just got off the phone with Immigration. They said they didn't receive your completed forms. I have to resubmit if they don't receive them in two months."

"John, I don't know what happen. Me go ta Lee's office today and find out what happen."

Early the next day, Gillian returned my call. "Lee was on vacation in America. When she return, she forgot about the application. Me give her one rass cussing. She say she complete the forms and take it ta Kingston Friday."

"I damn well hope so. It's been a year since we started the process. How much longer? Bring home my Gillian!"

Over the next year, the paperwork wended its way through the bureaucracies at a snail's pace. With all Gillian's medical and background checks carried out, I received a letter wanting another $800 to complete the final paperwork. The last hurdle before issuing Gillian her travel documents was an interview. Finally, all the documentation was completed, and it was time for Gillian to leave.

Flying to Jamaica at the end of August, I returned with Gillian on September 6, 1996. We were about to commence our new life together.

When we arrived in rural Ontario, Gillian was shocked. The countryside was desolate. Neighbors were a quarter to half a mile away. Gillian was accustomed to neighbors living within hailing distance. In Jamaica, the public transportation system serves urban as well as rural areas, while in Ontario, rural public transportation was nonexistent. Gillian didn't have the freedom to go where and when she wanted, as she had in Jamaica. She was dependent upon others for a ride.

The most stressful situation was her separation from her friends and family. Most of Gillian's immediate family, plus her aunts, uncles, and cousins, lived within a few miles of her. She interacted with them on a daily basis. Also, being the only Black person in the community was unsettling for her, as she faced racism she had never experienced at home.

At one point, when Gillian returned to Jamaica for a visit, she told her niece Sharon, "Me don't wanna return to Canada. Me miss everyone. Everythin' so different. Me lonely and sad."

"Ya can't leave Johnny. Him love ya. Thins will get better when ya make friends."

"Me go back, but if tings don't get better, me comin' home."

Upon her return, Gillian made the changes needed to adapt to the new lifestyle.

The first thing she needed was a driver's license if she wanted any degree of freedom. After studying the driver-training book, Gillian had no problem passing the beginner's test. Next, she signed up for a driver-training course. Whenever she went shopping or visiting with Mom or Anne, Gillian drove. Practice and more practice. She failed the driving test on her first attempt, but she succeeded on the second. I experienced a vicarious satisfaction when Gillian succeeded in obtaining her driver's license. Along with Gillian, I, too, would be gaining freedom.

Now that Gillian had a driver's license, she felt more comfortable. She could go where and when she wanted, but only if we could find a car. That was the next problem.

That's when a friend came to our rescue. Shimon, a close friend, inherited a relatively new car and an older beat-up Subaru. He gave us the Subaru, but we had to get the vehicle safety-checked. That could be expensive, but we caught another lucky break. My cousin Elmer was a mechanic with his own shop. He performed the safety check on the vehicle; all we did was pay for parts.

Because we bought used vehicles, Elmer became indispensable. It seemed that the old cars were constantly in need of repair. Elmer never charged for his labour; he only asked us to pay for parts. Without his kindness, we could never have kept a car on the road.

With Gillian's newfound freedom, she became more comfortable in her adopted home. At family parties and reunions, she became acquainted with my sisters, brothers, and cousins. As the number of Gillian's acquaintances increased, she began running into them when out. Slowly, she was beginning to feel a part of the community.

As the first year slipped by, a serious, festering problem came to a head.

"Your mother is always telling me what to do and how to do it," Gillian told me. "She tink me some little pickney that don't know what she doing. Me run a house in Jamaica fi years. Specky makes extra work. She clean windows, put them away in fall, and clean dem again when dem come out in spring. Dem not dirty. Just making work."

"I don't disagree, but where did you get the name Specky for her?"

"Because she is always inspecting what me do."

"Again, I will not disagree. Two women wanting to run the same house is pure trouble. I'll talk with Mom."

"Mom, Gillian says she doesn't like you always telling her what and how to do things."

"I'm only trying to teach her."

"I understand, but Gillian ran a household in Jamaica for years. She raised three of her nieces."

"But she has to learn where to shop, how to look after the water softener and appliances."

"You're right. The problem is not telling her where to shop, but when you tell her how to run the house. Running a house here is much like in Jamaica. Gillian is upset. If I have to move to keep her happy, I will."

With a tremor in her voice, Mom replied, "No, John! I don't want to cause that to happen. You couldn't afford to move. I won't cause you to do that."

Hugging Mom tightly, I whispered, "Don't cry. Things will work out. Remember telling me how you wanted to move to the senior citizen apartments in Formosa? You wanted a smaller place with no outdoor work. This is an ideal time for you and Frank to make the move."

"You're right, John. I've wanted to move for a couple of years. I'll talk it over with Frank."

After discussing the proposition for a few days, they decided to move. This took a few months, as they had to wait until an apartment became available. A moving party was arranged when the date to move was decided upon. All the neighbors attended the sendoff.

Before the move, we purchased some furniture and appliances, but we didn't take possession until Mom and Frank moved. At last, we were setting up our new home.

Now that Gillian was here, I could apply for a medical license to grow marijuana for my personal use. Prior to Gillian's arrival, a license was useless, as I couldn't go out to plant the marijuana. After the first season, Gillian's green thumb produced enough marijuana to help me control pain and sleep for the next year.

Until Gillian's arrival, I had smoked the weed, but this aggravated my breathing problems. The solution was simple. Gillian cooked the marijuana into brownies. I received the benefits of the marijuana without aggravating my breathing. Being married to Gillian was keeping me healthy.

Although the marijuana we grew was legal, every fall, the police used a helicopter to search for illegal weed. When the helicopter spotted some marijuana, they vectored a ground eradication team to the site. I knew what was about to happen when I heard the *whomp, whomp* of the helicopter as the downwash from the rotors shook the house.

Leaping into the wheelchair, I thought, "The fuckers are coming for my herb. Grab the license. I can't think straight with this horrible noise. Get out there before they rip up the plants."

Like a bullet, I shot outside into the drizzle, waving my license around, shouting, "I have a medical license! Don't touch my plants!"

The officer in charge said, "Let me see the license. I'll radio it in."

Meanwhile, the eradication team was searching the property, hoping to find some plants not covered by the license. By now, the helicopter pilot had spotted marijuana plants in the adjacent cornfield and was dropping dye markers so the eradication team could locate the plants.

Returning from his vehicle, the officer handed me the license, saying, "Everything checks out. I'll just slip out back here and look at your plants. Nice-looking crop, but you have one extra. I'll let it slide this time."

Finding nothing, they were soon on their way, but I couldn't stop shaking. The helicopter din and the police acting as if they were raiding the Hell's Angels clubhouse had my adrenaline pumping. Finally, I calmed down enough to stop shaking.

Upon her return, Gillian told me, "I heard you had company. You could see the copter for miles. They also left a mess under the pine trees along the road. It looks like they just dumped their Tim Horton coffee cups and wrappers under the trees when they got out of the vehicle. More work for me."

"Lucky I was here," I replied, "or the plants wouldn't be."

Although money was tight, Gillian was able to return to Jamaica for weddings or funerals. I had no problem coping when she was away. I popped the premade meals of chili, curried goat, and chicken stew into the microwave. I did dishes and wiped the counters and table. I took showers. I was self-sufficient, although upon Gillian's return, the toilet, table, and floor were not up to her high standards.

The worst part of Gillian's absence was the loneliness. While watching the news, I turned to the couch. "Gillian, that news story is sad."

Then I remembered. "You're not sitting on the couch. You're gone, but you'll soon return. Your absence is only temporary. What if it were permanent? I cringe at the thought. Giving my head a shake, I remember you'll be home in a few days, but the dark thoughts still haunt me."

After thirty years of total blindness, I was fully adapted to my situation. I accepted my blindness, not giving it a second thought, until a cyst formed on the cornea of my right eye.

For two years, I complained about the pain to my doctor, who constantly insisted, "There's nothing that can be done. Since you're blind, an ophthalmologist will not replace the cornea."

"But the pain is terrible sometimes. I feel like someone's driving a spike into my brain."

"You'll just have to put up with it."

One evening, when I could no longer endure the pain, I ended up at Emergency. The on-call doctor said, "I haven't seen an ulcerated eye in as bad a condition as yours before. I've phoned an ophthalmologist in Owen Sound, and they'll contact you tomorrow."

The next morning, after a two-hour drive, we arrived at the ophthalmologist's office. One look at the eye, and he told me, "You must have the eye operated on. I don't have the facilities here, but I'll arrange for an ophthalmologist in London to remove the eye. This is an emergency. I can't believe your doctor let it get to this point."

By noon the next day, we were at the Ivy Eye Clinic in London. While they prepped me for surgery, I asked the nurse, "Could I please have a drink of water? I've drunk nothing for the last twelve hours."

"Sorry. You can't have anything in your stomach when they sedate you."

"But nurse, they told me they wouldn't be sedating me."

"You're mistaken. We anesthetize all eye patients."

Sure enough, I was correct. No anesthesia, just some freezing around the eye and a bit of joy juice to relax me.

When I asked why, they told me, "It's because you're blind. You won't flinch when we approach your eye with a scalpel. Sighted people flinch."

I guess that's just one of the unexpected benefits of being blind. No more Johnny Cool. Now it's One-Eyed Jack.

With help from family and friends at Christmas and on birthdays, we scraped enough money together to start returning to Jamaica for two to three months in the winter. This time, we weren't returning to a house with no phone, water, or electricity. Gillian's uncle offered us the top floor of his rental house, rent-free. The money saved on heating paid for water, electricity, and taxis in Jamaica. For the next eight years, we visited every year, missing only two. By staying in Jamaica in the winter, I escaped all the snow and cold. My arthritis loved it.

24
Growing Old

On our return from Jamaica in 2016, the passenger behind me coughed and sniffled the entire trip. She was not the only one. At various locations on the plane, I heard more coughing and sniffles. I didn't give it a second thought.

A few days after our return, I noticed that I was downloading shows twice. I was also having difficulty remembering the key combinations for my screen-reading software. At one point, I couldn't remember how to turn off the computer.

I thought, "Not having internet access for three months while in Jamaica, you forgot how to download. Lack of use also caused you to forget some of the key combinations for the screen reader. No problem. After using the computer for a few more days, your dexterity will return."

I could not have been more wrong. A couple of days later, when John, a friend was visiting, I needed to use the toilet.

When sitting on the toilet, I gasped out, "John, I need help to get into the wheelchair. I can't get my breath. Help me pull up my pants. Get me a puffer (an inhaler). I'll be all right in a few minutes."

"No, you won't!" John vehemently exclaimed. "I'm phoning the ambulance. You can't breathe. You're not going to get better on your own."

Ignoring my feeble pleas, John phoned 911. When the ambulance arrived, the attendants didn't hesitate. They whisked me into the ambulance, slapped on an oxygen mask, and we were off to the hospital.

Upon entering the emergency room, I was suddenly the center of a flurry of medical activity. They inserted an IV port into the back of my hand, drew blood, and carried out a chest X-ray. After examining the X-ray, the doctor told me I had pneumonia. They immediately started an antibiotic IV drip. When all the procedures were completed, they left me alone while searching for a room. At that point, John, who had followed me to the hospital, came in to visit.

"I brought your book player. This will keep you busy until Gillian comes. Tell me what you need, and I'll tell Gillian. She can bring it when she comes to visit."

"All I can think of are my prescriptions, but I'm not thinking too clearly."

"I'm going back to your house. I'll wait for Gillian and tell her what happened. If she returns soon enough, I'll return to Perry Sound today. Get well. Phone me when you get out of the hospital."

"Thank you so much, John. I'm so glad you insisted on the hospital. Otherwise, I might have died."

When Gillian arrived, she found me still in one of the emergency treatment rooms. The staff had had a difficult time finding me a private room so I would be isolated in case the pneumonia was contagious. Gillian brought my prescriptions, but she didn't remain long. After helping me with soup and a sandwich, she departed for home and supper.

For the next few days, I floated along in a dream world. My thoughts were fuzzy. There was the never-ending hiss of life-giving oxygen. People came and went like ghosts in the night and IV drips were changed, but nothing seemed real.

Eating was difficult. Having no upper body support, I had to hold onto the bed rail for stability. That left me only one hand with which to eat. I needed help from Gillian or a nurse to eat. Sponge baths, diapers, drugs, and tender loving care got me through the next two weeks.

I wanted out of the hospital, but my fears loomed large. Could I still function at home? What changes to the house would I need to continue carrying on as before?

To help assuage my fears, the physiotherapy department arranged for me to get a booster seat for the toilet, a shower bench, and a side rail for the bed. Shortly after I returned home, a man delivered and installed my new equipment. The booster seat made getting on and off the toilet much less work. The shower bench was a necessity, since I could no longer get in and out of the tub by myself. I now depended on Gillian to give me a shower. I used the side rails to pull myself into a sitting position. After a few weeks, the side rails became more of a hindrance than a help. All these devices made less work for me, decreasing the demand on my lungs.

The biggest change was my attitude. I could no longer hurry. I told myself, "Slow and easy keeps you in the race. Too much excitement, and you need a puffer. In general, approach everything you do in a cool, calm manner. This will be difficult, as you are just an exuberant boy at heart."

After the bout of pneumonia, my doctor referred me to a respirologist.

The respirologist gave me a prescription for two inhalers. I used one daily and the other one during emergencies. When he gave me the prescriptions, he asked, "Do you have problems sleeping?"

"Yes! I don't get a sound sleep. I keep waking up. I feel like I'm drowning."

"You're suffering from sleep apnea. I'll schedule a sleep test for you. You'll come to the hospital in the evening, and they'll attach wires to your head. You then go to sleep. They record your brain activity while you sleep. There's also a camera recording your facial movements. I then read the results and write a prescription for a BiPAP machine. My secretary will get back to you with the sleep appointment. From now on, I want to see you twice a year."

The spell of pneumonia took a great deal out of me, leaving me more dependent. We still traveled to Jamaica, but now I had to carry the BiPAP machine and a shower bench.

Sitting for a long time was becoming more painful because of the worsening scoliosis. This meant that the two hours before flying, the four-hour flight, and the two-hour taxi ride to the house left me in agony. To try to mitigate the pain, I ate marijuana brownies before, during, and after the flight. At times, I supplemented the brownies with muscle relaxants, but I didn't like to, as they left my thought processes fuzzy.

On what would turn out to be my last trip to Jamaica, we had to leave the island earlier than expected. We had planned to stay until the end of March, but we escaped ten days earlier. Covid had commenced its ruthless rampage.

During January and February of 2020, Covid was seldom in the Jamaican news. However, when March arrived, the disease became a hot topic. Friends and family in Canada advised us to come home as quickly as possible. This meant Gillian had to scramble. She had to have a set of dentures made and fitted. She needed some things from the market and grocery store. Finally, it was time to depart.

When traveling, I took all possible precautions to ensure I did not contract the virus. With my respiratory problems, Covid could be a death sentence. I wore a stocking cap, sunglasses, and a mask. I was protecting my ears, eyes, nose, and mouth.

The airport was in chaos. The Covid scare had everyone in a state of fear. No one seemed to know what was going on, not even the staff.

An attendant who was helping us told me, "Take off the mask. People think you have Covid. They're all shying away from you."

I thought, "This is crazy. The mask is supposed to prevent a person from getting Covid. It doesn't mean you have Covid."

To appease the woman, I temporarily lowered the mask, but I always kept my mouth covered.

Because of the chaotic racket, I felt isolated. The clamour around me was a blur of sound. I could only understand someone if they shouted directly into my ear.

On the airplane, I felt sorry for our seatmate. She sat in the window seat, and if she could have crawled onto the wing to avoid me, I'm certain she would have. I think the mask terrified her, as it frightened the attendant. Everyone assumed I had the virus.

Disembarking at the Toronto airport, we faced a completely different scenario. It was quiet, with very few travelers. All the staff wore masks, gloves, and protective suits. The immigration screening was perfunctory, and the customs check was nonexistent. I wished I had brought four bottles of cognac instead of only one. Everyone received a pamphlet on

Covid and reminders that quarantining was mandatory.

Luckily, I never contracted the Covid virus.

That was my last trip to Jamaica. The trip was becoming too painful for me and strenuous for Gillian. When we traveled through the airport, an attendant pushed me, but Gillian felt like a donkey, laden with the BiPAP machine, her carry-on bag, the laptop bag, and her purse. All I held was my murse and carry-on bag. However, I didn't feel bad, as Covid kept everyone at home. Even when Covid cases dropped, flying remained difficult because of the restrictions.

In 2021, once again I rode to the hospital in an ambulance.

Four days prior to that, I received the Covid vaccine. A few days later, when transferring to the treatment bed for an ultrasound, I had difficulty breathing. Two days later, when getting out of bed, I used my emergency inhaler twice. Just before breakfast, I needed another shot of Ventolin, my emergency inhaler. Getting on the toilet was the catalyst that sent me to the hospital. I could not transfer back to the wheelchair without Gillian's aid. Even using the emergency puffers, I still gasped for air.

This time, when the ambulance arrived, the attendants pulled on rubber gloves, masks, and protective plastic suits over their clothes. At the hospital, I endured a swab test for Covid. After checking the chest X-ray, the doctor told me I had pneumonia.

"Not again," I groaned.

"I'm afraid so. After one case of pneumonia, you become more susceptible to it."

When I heard that, I knew what was in store for me: IV antibiotic drips, oxygen, steroids, and puffers. The major difference between this hospital stay and the previous one was all the Covid protocols. On my previous hospital stay, I had had company almost every day. This time, Gillian was the only person allowed to visit. At least this was a shorter hospital stay than the previous one, as I was out in a week.

It seemed that with every hospital visit, I lost a little more of my independence. By this point, I only sat for an hour for breakfast and a couple of hours for supper. No more trips to Jamaica. Fewer visits to friends, because sitting for the car ride became more painful. Medical appointments became my major outing. We needed a vehicle that had seats that fully reclined so I could lie down.

Being unable to visit as I had in the past, I quickly learned who my true friends were. Those that were more than acquaintances continued to drop in for a visit. Some brought beer to enliven our conversation. We played games. They did jobs around the house that neither Gillian nor I could manage. Their visits gave me something to look forward to. They helped keep me interested in life. I learned that true friends are more valuable than anything except life itself.

I could no longer slide down hillsides in the rain, shower in a dishpan, snowmobile, or stay in other countries. My days of wild adventuring were over. I continued to visit with friends, read, and use the computer, but something was missing. In the past, going to university, smuggling, meeting Gillian, and getting her to Canada gave me purpose. I no longer had a purpose. I felt empty.

What could I do to restore meaning to my life? I thought and thought, and then it came to me. "If you can no longer seek out adventure, you can write about it. You've talked about writing your life story. Do it! This is your chance to pay tribute to the three most important women in your life, your mother, Anne, and Gillian. Maybe, because you never gave up no matter what misfortune befell you, your story will give hope to others.

You have the skills, but you need help and an audience."

After reading *Behind Our Eyes*, the second literary anthology of stories, poems, and essays by writers with disabilities, edited by Kate Chamberlin, I knew I had found a home when I joined BOE in 2022. Members read my stories, making suggestions on how to improve the prose. Winslow, one of the members, gave me help with editing and using JAWS for proofreading stories. Having written essays all my life, assistance from BOE members was indispensable in teaching me the art of story writing. I now had a goal.

One of the first stories I wrote after joining the group documented another trip to the hospital with severe breathing problems. This was my third trip to the hospital in six years, and the worst breathing episode.

When preparing for a family reunion, I tried different seating arrangements for my new travel chair. As I switched back and forth, I needed to use the toilet. Transferring to the toilet turned out to be too much work in too short a time. The demand on my lungs was too much. I could no longer get a deep breath to expel the CO_2. All I could manage was short, rapid, rabbit-like breaths. I couldn't get off the toilet without assistance. Gillian wiped me, helped me into the chair, and dialed 911. The ambulance took forever; at least, that was how it felt as I fought for every breath.

This time, I didn't have pneumonia, although I still ended up in an isolation ward. As was the case with the previous hospital visit, the Covid protocols were still in effect. This meant that Gillian was my only visitor, and I had to endure a Covid swab shoved up my nose. No antibiotic IV, but I received drugs to relax me, as blood was drawn every hour. They wanted to monitor certain chemical markers they found in my blood along with the oxygen. The chemical markers indicated some heart damage, but later, they determined that no damage had occurred.

Two days passed before they found me a room. When Gillian finally found me after the move, she brought me my laptop. Now I could write. After Gillian departed, I immediately started typing my story, as there was very little else to do

I needed help to sit and eat. Choking was a constant concern. After six days, a physiotherapist brought me a two-kilogram dumbbell (4.4 lbs.) so I could rebuild my strength. He also helped me transfer from the bed to the wheelchair. Remaining in the wheelchair for lunch, I could feed myself at last.

After a few more days, I no longer needed oxygen. With Gillian's help, I could transfer from bed to wheelchair. Since I was able to handle these basic tasks, the doctor agreed to discharge me. Eight days after arriving in an ambulance, I was finally going home.

On my return, with Gillian's help, I was able to use the toilet and shower the next day. I was happy that I hadn't lost more of my ability to do things. However, I found myself becoming anxious when approaching certain tasks. This made my breathing worse. I needed to remember to stay calm, never rush, and not worry.

I noticed that after eating a brownie before supper, my breathing improved. On my next visit to the respirologist, I wanted to ask him if marijuana would help open my bronchial passages.

A couple of months after I was discharged from the hospital, I had a visit with my respirologist. My first question for him was, "About 30 or 45 minutes after eating a marijuana brownie, my breathing seems to improve. Is the brownie opening up my airways?"

"No. They've carried out trials, but there is no evidence that marijuana improves breathing. The brownie helps to relax you, lessening any stress you might have, which helps to keep the airways open. If you feel it helps, continue using it.

"Now, I want to talk about your last stay in the hospital. It sounds like you had a life-threatening episode. I'm glad there was no heart damage."

"Why were my oxygen numbers in the safe range, but I still fought for every breath?" I asked.

"When a person breathes in, the oxygen goes into the bloodstream, and they expel the CO_2. Because you have weak lungs, you have difficulty expelling all the CO_2. It collects in the bottom of the lungs because your shallow breaths don't expel the CO_2 completely. It builds up until you wake, feeling as if you're drowning. During this last episode, you didn't expel the CO_2, so you felt like you were drowning, even though you were taking in oxygen. That's why they put you on a BiPAP machine at the hospital. It cycles air into your lungs and draws out the CO_2."

"I think I understand. By the way, I've had problems with the BiPAP machine. At times I wake, feeling like I'm drowning."

"I'll change the prescription for the machine. Just take the machine and the prescription to the same place you get the masks. I'm also giving you a prescription for an antibiotic that will help break up phlegm. Take it Monday, Wednesday, and Friday. See you in six months."

A big improvement to my life was the 2017 Mazda our nephew Nick helped us purchase. The front seat fully reclines, allowing me to lie flat when traveling. This makes travel a pleasure instead of a pain.

As I've grown older, a car that I can lie flat in has become indispensable. Otherwise, pain increases and my independence decreases. Virtually everyone will lose some of their freedom as they grow older.

Now that I've completed my memoir, what can I do to give purpose to my life? I can publish and peddle my story. I could approach local libraries to see if they want to host a book signing. There is always hope that another book lurks in me, just waiting for release.

I hear people say they couldn't live a restricted life like mine. I tell them, "Wait until you grow older and tasks become more difficult. Eyesight goes, teeth wear out, and in general, the old body falls apart. I know some people who can't accept the loss as they age, becoming miserable. Some may even contemplate suicide. Not this boy. Life is too precious to surrender. I can still read, write, visit with friends, think, and try to make a better world. I'll give up when I'm in the ground."

When I was growing up, Mom told me, "Smile, and the world smiles with you. Weep, and you weep alone." Through all the difficulties in my life, I have always tried to live by that motto, but I never could have made it without Mom, Gillian, Anne, Frank, and friends. The love of others is what makes life worthwhile.

About the Author

John Walter Cronin was born in 1955 and was adopted at six months by a farming family in Ontario, Canada. At the age of four, he contracted polio, which left him a paraplegic.

Understanding that he needed a good education if he wanted to succeed, John attended the University of Waterloo. It was there in the late 1970s and early '80s that he obtained his bachelor's and master's degrees. His main areas of study were metaphysics, epistemology, ethics, and politics.

After becoming blind due to RP (retinitis pigmentosa), he began to travel, living in Alberta, Texas, and Jamaica. John met Gillian White in Jamaica, where they married in 1993.

John enjoys reading, writing, and sharing interesting conversations with longtime friends over a beer.

Website:
www.dldbooks.com/johncronin/

Email: crow2k55@hotmail.com

Manufactured by Amazon.ca
Bolton, ON

45836615R00118